Soccer and Racism

Soccer and Racism

The Beginnings of *Futebol* in São Paulo and Rio de Janeiro, 1895–1933

By Rosana Barbosa

ANTHEM PRESS

Anthem Press
An imprint of Wimbledon Publishing Company
www.anthempress.com

This edition first published in UK and USA 2022
by ANTHEM PRESS
75–76 Blackfriars Road, London SE1 8HA, UK
or PO Box 9779, London SW19 7ZG, UK
and
244 Madison Ave #116, New York, NY 10016, USA

Copyright © Rosana Barbosa 2022

The author asserts the moral right to be identified as the author of this work.

British Library Cataloguing-in-Publication Data
A catalogue record for this book is available from the British Library.

Library of Congress Control Number: 2022934145

ISBN-13: 978-1-83998-475-4 (Hbk)
ISBN-10: 1-83998-475-9 (Hbk)

ISBN-13: 978-1-78527-924-9 (Pbk)
ISBN-10: 1-78527-924-6 (Pbk)

This title is also available as an e-book.

CONTENTS

Foreword   vii

Introduction   1

1   Soccer and Investments as Civilizing Forces   9

    The Early Years of Soccer in São Paulo and Rio de Janeiro   9

    Urban Development in São Paulo and Rio de Janeiro   16

    The Brazilian, Traction, Power and Light Company   17

    The Light and *Futebol* in São Paulo   20

2   Racial Exclusion in the Gentleman's Sport   25

    Rio's *Liga Metropolitana*   25

    The South American Cup of 1921   28

3   Soccer and Lusophobia   37

    The Portuguese as an Immigrant Group and Lusophobia   37

    Club de Regatas Vasco da Gama and the Associação
        Metropolitana de Esportes Atléticos (AMEA)   40

    Amateurism versus Professionalism   46

Epilogue: The End of Exclusion but the Continuation of Racism   49

Bibliography   53

Index   61

FOREWORD

In this book, Rosana Barbosa provides an innovative and deeply insightful interpretive discussion of the role of soccer as an instrument of change in Brazil. Sport historians have assessed and debated for many years the nature of the process of sport diffusion—how a sport can travel from one country to another, and the changes that it undergoes in adapting socially and culturally to the new location. National historians of various countries in the world, or those at least who are inclined toward integrating social and cultural history into their narratives, have recognized that sport can be a sensitive reflector of societal characteristics as well as serving at times as a way of asserting national and political identity. Both of these approaches are valid, and yet this study goes further than either of them. Dr. Barbosa shows in compelling detail the way in which the transformation of *football* into *futebol* intersected in Brazil, in the period from 1895 to 1933, with the evolution and partial resolution of crucial issues involving racialization and the search for social cohesion. Sport, in this case, was not just a cultural expression in the throes of change—though it was that—and not just a barometer of broader social transmutations—though it was that too—but rather it was a key agent of change. For the historian, soccer in this era is also shown in the book to offer a revealing lens through which to draw analytical conclusions about Brazilian society in the broadest sense.

The introduction of soccer to Brazil came through British economic connections that were already longstanding by the late nineteenth century, and notably at the level of the elite capital-owning class in São Paulo as well as at that of a humbler artisanal working class in the suburbs of Rio de Janeiro. But what made the sport a potentially volatile insertion into Brazilian society was its rapid assimilation into ongoing intellectual and social struggles over the distribution of power and primacy in a Brazil that was undergoing economic expansion and urbanization, and especially over its racialized identity. Not only did Brazil have a substantial Afro-Brazilian population that differentiated it from, say, Argentina, but also prevailing pseudo-scientific racism maintained that even the Portuguese—the originators of settler colonialism in Brazil, and also the source of a major late nineteenth-century immigration—were themselves of questionable racial quality by comparison with their more northern European neighbours. For a Brazilian elite wrestling with such questions, the gentlemanly values supposedly associated with a British sport represented an opportunity to demonstrate the noble qualities associated with a thoroughly racialized concept of refinement. However, a diffused sport is always unlikely to follow anyone's convenient agenda, and the growth of working-class soccer—especially, though not exclusively, in Rio—soon presented a crucial challenge. This was exemplified by the rise in Rio of the Vasco da Gama club, an outgrowth of a rowing club founded by recent Portuguese immigrants and soon seeking out Afro-Brazilian players who could give the team a level of skill and commitment that carried it to its first national championship in 1923.

From these elements, and weaving in debates over professionalism as well as related efforts to obstruct the careers of racialized and working-class players through literacy and occupational tests, Dr. Barbosa has crafted a clear portrayal of the dynamic between sport and society. Exclusion on class and racial grounds was ultimately overturned by the early 1930s—though not in its gendered form, as shown by the obstacles still faced by women's soccer—and the populist President Getúlio Vargas publicly embraced the concept of a mixed-race national team as a symbol of Brazilian identity. So, for the men at least, inclusion now prevailed. But Dr. Barbosa scrupulously avoids making this a story of triumphalism. Racism was still routinely experienced even by the great players of a later generation such as Pelé and Garrincha. Thus, this is a book characterized not only by analytical insight, but also by nuance and sensibility. It is a vivid study in sport history and in Brazilian history, and—most importantly—a demonstration of the inseparability of both during a crucial era.

John Reid
Saint Mary's University

INTRODUCTION

This book uses soccer as a tool to explain key elements of Brazil's history from the downfall of the monarchy to the 1930 revolution, or what is known as the First Republic. The book covers the period from 1895, when the first official game based on British Football Association rules was organized, to the professionalization of the sport in 1933, with a focus on the cities of São Paulo and Rio de Janeiro.[1] Overall, this book demonstrates that the advent of soccer in Brazil and the reaction of the elites toward this sport can be understood primarily as a consequence of the desire of the new Republic—crucially influenced by Social Darwinism—to be included within the white, "civilized" countries. Thus, racism during the early years of *football* was influenced by Eurocentric views of the world, in racial terms, and the Brazilian elites' desire to be accepted by these countries.

In addition, this book furthers the discussion of the racist/elitist beginnings of soccer in Brazil by connecting the exclusions to the racist ideas shaped by Social Darwinism that took place.[2] Despite the fact that the "snobbish" beginnings of soccer in Brazil are well examined in the historiography, the reasons for this are not well explained: It is simply viewed as a natural consequence of the post-abolition period. The book's focus on racial exclusion intends to show that color discrimination was a reality in the country, but it does not ignore the socioeconomic barriers that existed and that affected the poor in general.

The research for the book was based on newspapers and secondary sources, mostly in Portuguese. The study aims to be short and accessible to non-experts on Brazil who may be interested in reading it because of their interest in soccer. In fact, the book grew out of an undergraduate course that was offered at Saint Mary's University in 2014—just before the World Cup—that

---

1 Not to be confused with the two states that bear the same name.
2 For a better understanding of Social Darwinism, see Robert W Sussman, *The Myth of Race: The Troubling Persistence of an Unscientific Idea* (Cambridge: Harvard University Press, 2014).

examined Brazilian history through the evolution of soccer. This course was initially expected to be offered only once as a special topic, but the interest in it was so high that it became part of the university calendar, and it continues to attract students from all faculties. In March 2014, the course's impact also resonated in the broader community when the *Huffington Post* listed it as one of the "coolest classes in Canada."[3] Students from this course are the inspiration for this book.

Football arrived in Brazil in the last decade of the nineteenth century during a time of transition after the abolition of slavery in 1888 and the overthrow of the Orleans de Bragança imperial family in 1889, which had ruled the country since its independence from Portugal in 1822. A Republican government was installed with a clear desire to modernize and Europeanize Brazil. This aspiration was a challenging one, because for about 300 years, Brazil had been a major receiver of enslaved Africans, and their significant presence hindered plans for creating a nation of white people. Although formal color segregation was never practiced, Brazilian society at the turn of the twentieth century was elitist, with whites (or fair-skinned individuals) dominating and disempowering most of the population.

It was during the First Republic that a more systematic racism began to develop. During that time, non-European cultural expressions, such as capoeira (a type of martial arts), the Afro-Brazilian religion of candomblé and samba, were even more repressed than in the past. Capoeira was even prohibited under the country's 1890 criminal code. The impoverished population (of which the majority were non-whites) was also excluded from any political participation, although legally, every Brazilian was equal. The constitution of the new Republic, promulgated in 1891, disenfranchised people who were illiterate while exempting the federal government from funding and overseeing public education by making it the responsibility of the states of the new Republic. Needless to say, public education was not a priority and thus Brazilian society was highly stratified.[4] The richest state at the time, São Paulo, only began to "construct the rudiments of an elementary school system" in 1900, and public secondary education was not widely available until the 1920s.[5] Thus, a variety of political and institutional structures sustained the idea of the inferiority of non-whites and guaranteed white domination of

---

3 http://www.huffingtonpost.ca/2014/09/03/coolest-classescanada_n_5755176.html

4 Nancy Stepan, *The Hour of Eugenics: Race, Gender, and Nation in Latin America* (Ithaca: Cornell University Press, 1996), 37. See also Jerry Dávila, *Diploma of Whiteness: Race and Social Policy in Brazil* (Durham: Duke University Press), 2003.

5 George Reid Andrews, *Blacks & Whites in São Paulo, Brazil, 1888-1988* (Madison: The University of Wisconsin Press, 1991), 72.

society, not so much through laws but, rather, through inherited norms and patterns of behaviour.[6]

This period also witnessed an unprecedented increase in immigration due to an intensive campaign to attract settlers and workers. Overall, Brazil received about 4.5 million immigrants between 1821 and 1932,[7] breaking records for newcomers in the 1890s and early 1900s. Under the influence of racist ideas, which justified white colonization and domination over non-white settlers, Europe was seen as a model and European immigration as a tool for decreasing the predominance of non-whites in the population. Most Brazilians, like others in the Americas, believed that white was better, and the elite praised the superior qualities of Northern Europeans and generally accepted the idea of "Aryan superiority" as a historical fact.[8] Thus, in 1890, a governmental decree barred the immigration of Asians and Africans, who could be admitted to the country only under specific conditions and by permission of the National Congress.[9]

This decree was a natural consequence of the upper echelons' misgivings about their own racial inferiority, a fact that tormented Brazilian elites. The ideas of Social Darwinism, as deduced from English, French, and German sources, were especially influential in Brazil, and several debates took place in the last decades of the nineteenth century about the "inferiority" of the mixed-race population and the possible solutions to this "problem." European intellectuals who defended the notion of white superiority had no hesitation in pointing out how Brazil had serious racial inadequacies due to its large population of Africans and their descendants.[10] For example, the Swiss-born American biologist Louis Agassiz (who had lived in Brazil between 1865 and 1866) claimed that "[t]hese who try to deny the pernicious effects of racial mixing [...] should come to Brazil [...] no one can deny that miscegenation

---

6 Charles W. Mills, *Blackness Visible: Essays on Philosophy and Race* (Ithaca: Cornell University Press, 1998), 101–2.

7 Eduardo José Míguez, "Introduction," in *Mass Migration to Modern Latin America*, ed. Samuel Baily and Eduardo José Míguez (Wilmington: A Scholarly Resources Inc, 2003), XIV.

8 Jessica Lynn Graham, *Shifting the Meaning of Democracy. Race, Politics, and Culture in the United States and Brazil* (Oakland: University of California Press, 2019), 11–12; and Thomas Skidmore, *Black into White. Race and Nationality in Brazilian Thought* (New York: Duke University Press, 1998 – 2nd edition, 3rd printing), 52–53.

9 Skidmore, *Black into White*, 137. See also: Graham, *Shifting*, 12–13.

10 Regina Horta Duarte, *Activist Biology. The National Museum, Politics, and Nation Building in Brazil* (Tucson: The University of Arizona Press, 2016), 31; and Stepan, *The Hour*, 41 & 45.

shuts down the best qualities of each race."[11] A few years later, the French writer and diplomat Arthur Gobineau claimed that no "Brazilian has pure blood" and that racial mixing "had produced the most pitiful degeneration, both in the lower as in the upper classes."[12] In the early twentieth century, a British newspaper published in São Paulo pointed out that the former British ambassador to the United States had claimed that Brazil had some "disadvantages, chiefly racial" that caused backwardness.[13]

Thus, the main concern to decision-makers in Brazil was to convince the international community that the country was not doomed racially. Subsequently, European immigration and miscegenation were seen as ways to refute the predictions of Brazil being a racially inadequate country.[14] It was claimed that miscegenation between whites and fair-skinned Brazilians would whiten the country to the point that—as was claimed by the physician João Baptista Lacerda in the London Universal Races Congress in 1911—Blacks in Brazil would be extinct by the early twenty-first century (in 2012, according to his calculations). He believed that light-skinned and white individuals would produce a bright, healthy population and that the "deeply degenerate populations" would breed with each other, accelerating "their extinction, as a result of their progressive decadence."[15] Lacerda was trying to persuade the international community that, with time, Brazil would appear whiter and would therefore civilize itself. Miscegenation would create people who were almost as developed as whites,[16] despite the general assumption in Europe

---

11 Juanma Arteaga, "Biological Discourses on Human Races and Scientific Racism in Brazil (1832–1911)," *Journal of the History of Biology* 50, no. 2 (2017): 280.
12 Arteaga, "Biological," 279.
13 *The Brazilian Review*, December 17, 1912.
14 Brian Owensby, "Toward a History of Brazil's 'Cordial Racism': Race Beyond Liberalism," *Society for Comparative Study of Society and History*, 47, no. 2 (2005): 326–7. See also: Giralda Seyferth, "Construindo a Nação: Hierarquias Raciais e o Papel do Racismo na Política de Imigração e Colonização," in *Raça, Ciência e Sociedade*, org. Macus Chor Maio & Ricardo Ventura Santos (Rio de Janeiro: Scielo Books, 1996), 43; and Nisia Trindade Lima & Gilberto Hochman, "Condenado pela Raça, Absolvido pela Medicina: O Brasil Descoberto pelo Movimento Sanitarista da Primeira República," in *Raça, Ciência e Sociedade*, org. Macus Chor Maio & Ricardo Ventura Santos (Rio de Janeiro: Scielo Books, 1996), 27.
15 Arteaga, "Biological," 300.
16 Antonio Sérgio Alfredo Guimarães, "Racism and Anti-Racism in Brazil: A Postmodern Perspective," in: *Racism and Anti-racism in World Perspective*, ed. Benjamin P. Bowser (Thousand Oaks: Sage Publications, 1995), 218; Lilia Moritz Schwarcz, *O Espetáculo das Raças. Cientistas, Instituições e Questão Racial no Brasil – 1870-1930* (São Paulo: Companhia das Letras, 1993), 25 & 54; and Skidmore, *Black into White*, 44–6.

and North America that racial mixing should be condemned due to its supposed deterioration of the "superior" race.

It was precisely this idea that was disseminated by José Custodio Alves de Lima, who had been a member of the Brazilian Commission at the Saint Louis International Exposition in 1905. Lima explicitly asked the *Brazilian Review*, a British paper published in Rio, to print a letter that he had written criticizing Theodore Roosevelt and his corollary to the Monroe Doctrine, which claimed the United States as the "protector" of the Americas. He stated that Roosevelt had no right to dictate how Latin Americans should manage their affairs. In the letter, Lima defended Brazil on racial terms, but in doing so, he exposed his own racism. He claimed that Brazil was doing quite well and that the country had no racial prejudices. His reasoning for stating this was the fact that the Black "element is fast disappearing by the process of elimination, by simply being in contact with a more intelligent and stronger race." In this way, he denied Brazil's racial inadequacies and pointed out that "the law of the survival of the fittest is making its way smoothly and naturally."[17]

Thus, a whitened Brazil was just a matter of time, and while dark-skinned people would not disappear, they were to be kept hidden as much as possible. Within this context, cities began sponsoring urban reform initiatives, pushing impoverished dark-skinned individuals away from the downtown area. This impact was seen mostly in the capital of the country, Rio de Janeiro, which went through major urban reforms. It was during this period that shanty towns—the *favelas*—began to appear as a consequence of this dislocation of the poor from the central region of major cities; their former neighborhoods gave way to Parisian-style avenues and buildings in the core.[18] As elsewhere, this beautification process resulted in the eviction of thousands of families, pushing them away, as if hiding its poor and non-white citizens would automatically give Brazil the veneer of "civilization."[19]

---

17 *The Brazilian Review*, October 31, 1905.

18 Today, the majority of the residents of the favelas are still Blacks and mixed-race people, who struggle to break the social barriers imposed since the time of slavery. https://www.ibge.gov.br/estatisticas/sociais/populacao/25844-desigualdades-sociais-por-cor-ou-raca.html?=&t=publicacoes and https://www.creditas.com/exponencial/negros-desigualdade-social/

19 Mary Del Priore, *Histórias da Gente Brasileira*, Volume 3, República—Memórias, 1889–1950 (Rio de Janeiro: Editora Casa da Palavra, 2017), 20; Brodwyn Fischer, *A Poverty of Rights. Citizenship and Inequality in Twentieth-Century Rio de Janeiro* (Stanford: Stanford University Press, 2008), 31–8; Nicolau Sevcenko, *Literatura Como Missão. Tensões sociais e criação cultural na Primeira República* (São Paulo: Editora Brasiliense, 1983), 33. See also: Romulo Mattos, "Shantytown Dwellers' Resistance in Brazil's

Although Brazil was never part of the British empire, Great Britain had a significant influence in the country throughout the nineteenth century. This process began in 1808, when the British assisted the Portuguese government to transfer to its main colony in order to escape a Napoleonic invasion and possible takeover. From that point forward, the country became one of the main markets for British products. The British also provided loans and invested in infrastructure that they controlled, including railroads, sewer systems and telegraph companies. British dominance remained almost untouched until after World War I.[20]

Alongside these investments, a specialized labor force from Britain arrived in the country. These professionals were seen as agents of modernity who would contribute to Brazil's progress and rise to prominence due to the strength and superiority of the empire's *raça saxônica*.[21] In this context, *football* was seen as an instrument of civilization. It was not that the British were imposing sports on the elites of Brazil; rather, the elites sought to adopt the traditions and pastimes of British culture and imitate them in order to gain a sense of superiority.[22] As an English-language newspaper from Buenos Aires noted, the British were the best soccer players because they were a superior race.[23]

British *Footballers* took pride in the expansion of soccer in the world, as if they could influence other people to learn from the superior Anglo-Saxons'

First Republic (1890–1930): Fighting for the Right of the Poor to Reside in the City of Rio De Janeiro," *International Labor and Working Class History*, no. 83 (2013): 54–69.

20 Rosana Barbosa, *Brazil and Canada. Economic, Political, and Migratory Ties, 1820s to 1970s* (Laham: Lexington Books, 2017), XIV–XV & 6. For more information on the transfer of the Royal government, see Patrick Wilcken, *Empire Adrift. The Portuguese Court in Rio de Janeiro, 1808-1821* (London: Bloomsbury, 2004); and Kirsten Schultz, *Tropical Versailles: Empire Monarchy, and the Portuguese Royal Court in Rio de Janeiro, 1808-1821* (New York: Routledge, 2001).

21 André Ricardo Maciel Botelho, "Da Geral à Tribuna, da Redação ao Espetáculo: A Imprensa Esportiva e a Popularização do Futebol (1900-1920)," in *Memória Social dos Esportes. Futebol e Política: A Construção de uma Identidade Nacional*, org. por Francisco Carlos Teixeira da Silva and Ricardo Pinto dos Santos (Rio de Janeiro: Mauade Editora: FAPERJ, 2006), 325; and *Correio da Manhã*, 1 de maio de 1908.

22 J. A. Mangan. "Prologue: Emulation, Adaptation and Serendipity," *The International Journal of the History of Sport*, 18, no. 3 (2001): 2 and Matthew Brown. "British informal empire and the origins of association football in South America," *Soccer and Society*, 16, no. 2–3 (2015): 173–4.

23 *The Buenos Aires Herald*, May 23, 1909, cited by Phil Vasili, *Colouring over the White Line. The History of Black Footballers in Britain* (Edinburgh and London: Mainstream Publishing, 2000), 46.

values.[24] In 1903, the *Brazilian Review* stated that "British energy is inextinguishable and foot-ball flourishes even on the Equator, a club having been lately formed at Pará" (located in the north of Brazil, near Amazonas state).[25] In the British Caribbean, C. L. R. James described how it took him many years to understand what had been imposed on him and others, that "Britain was the source of all light and leading, and our business was to admire, wonder, imitate, learn; our criterion of success was to have succeeded in approaching that distant ideal—to attain it was, of course, impossible."[26]

Thus, the large British community in Brazil would have a significant effect on the beginnings of *football*, and the racial assumptions of these Europeans was a major influencing factor on the beginnings of that sport in the country. Europeans—especially Anglo-Saxons—considered Brazilians to be racially inferior, or "ineligible for membership in the White men's club" due to their Portuguese ancestry and their mixed-race origin.[27] The Portuguese, it should be noted, were also considered to be non-whites, and therefore also inferior to the British.[28] As James stated about a cricket team in Trinidad, the only white man that had joined the team was a Trinidadian-born Portuguese, "which did not count exactly as white (unless very wealthy)."[29]

As previously noted, this book covers the period from 1895, when the first known organized game happened in São Paulo, to 1933, when soccer became democratized with the advent of professionalization. It is divided into three chapters and an epilogue. Chapter 1, "Soccer and Investments as Civilizing Forces," looks at the turn of the century, when organized soccer began to be played in a systematic way by the European community of Rio and São Paulo. It demonstrates that the new sport was embraced by these people as a way to celebrate their culture. Young, wealthy Brazilians also embraced soccer as a way of participating in a trendy European sport that was identified with a respected, white/upper-class activity and also as a way to distinguish themselves from the "lower" and darker populations. Making this distinction was important in this moment of post-emancipation, as it affirmed the

---

24 Phil Vasili, *The First Black Footballer. Arthur Wharton, 1865-1930. An Absence of Memory* (Portland: Frank Cass Publishers, 1998), 78.

25 *The Brazilian Review*, October 20, 1903.

26 C. L. R. James, *Beyond a Boundary* (London: Yellow Jersey Press, 1963), 39.

27 Marilyn Lake and Henry Reynolds, *Drawing the Global Colour Line: White Men's Countries and the International Challenge of Racial Equality. Critical Perspectives on Empire* (Cambridge: Cambridge University Press, 2008), 198.

28 Lourenço Cardoso, *O Branco ante a rebeldia do desejo: um estudo sobre a branquitude no Brasil* (Tese Doutoramento, UNESP/Araraquara, 2014), 27.

29 James, *Beyond*, 65.

superiority of the white upper classes. In the colonial mentality, it was also important for the European residents of Rio and São Paulo to distinguish themselves from Brazilians. As well, *football* was one aspect of modernity that these two cities were craving to achieve.

Chapter 2, "Racial Exclusion in the Gentlemen's Sport," demonstrates how, because *football* began as an upper-class activity, the lower classes—especially dark-skinned individuals—were excluded from it until the late 1920s/early 1930s. Indeed, the chapter highlights how soccer provides two rare examples of color segregation in Brazil.

Chapter 3, "Soccer and Lusophobia," continues to highlight the impact of European-based racial assumptions on the development of professional soccer. The struggle to keep the sport amateur was a direct consequence of the attempt to make racial and social distinctions within Brazil. The chapter specifically looks at the role of Clube de Regatas Vasco da Gama in the professionalization process. The club was an example of the influence of the ideas defended by racism, as the Portuguese (or Lusos) were considered an inferior European type, often regarded by other Europeans as non-whites.

The epilogue considers how national discourse after 1930 was one of reconciliation, of formulating a new Brazilian identity attributable to Brazil's racial mixing. These ideas had their roots in artists and intellectuals but was soon embraced by politicians under the leadership of President Getúlio Vargas. Although this attitude led to the fall of class and racial barriers within soccer, the same could not be said for racism in other domains of life, nor did Brazil become a racial democracy. The latter notion has been repeated by many contemporaries and reinforced by the military dictatorship that ruled Brazil from 1964 to 1985, but with the drafting of a new Constitution in 1988 returning Brazil to a democracy, this idea began to be disputed and is nowadays discredited.[30]

---

30 For more information, see Jerry Dávila, "Brazilian Race Relations in the Shadow of Apartheid," *Radical History Review* 2014, no. 119 (2014): 123 & 132–3. See also Fischer, *A Poverty*, 306. For the 1940s, see Graham, *Shifting*, 243–4.

Chapter 1

SOCCER AND INVESTMENTS AS CIVILIZING FORCES

The Early Years of Soccer in São Paulo and Rio de Janeiro

Ball games that resembled soccer began being played in Brazil in the second half of the nineteenth century, mainly at schools as a way to discipline young men.[1] Yet soccer based on the rules of British Association Football only arrived in Brazil due to the actions of European residents—mostly the British, their descendants, and their wealthy Brazilian friends. The small but tightly connected British community was closely related to the Brazilian elite, for whom *football* was much more than a sport: it was a symbol of modernity and civilization.

Two names that come to light in this process are Thomas Donohoe and Charles Miller.[2] Donohoe was a Scot born in Busby, near Glasgow, who left for Brazil in May 1894 to work as a master dyer at the Companhia Progresso Industrial in Bangu, a suburb of Rio de Janeiro. This textile factory was inaugurated in 1892 and relied on British machines and technicians. Although very little is known about Donohoe, it seems that his wife brought a soccer ball when she and their two sons joined him in Brazil, months after his arrival. Donohoe began organizing informal soccer games right away with his British co-workers, sometimes with teams comprising six players on each side due to the lack of British residents in Bangu to form two full teams. The

---

1 Fatima Martin Rodrigues Ferreira Antunes, "O Futebol de Fábrica em São Paulo" (Dissertação de Mestrado em Sociologia. Departamento de Sociologia da Faculdade de Filosofia, Letras e Ciências Humanas da Universidade de São Paulo, 1992), 16.

2 Agnaldo Kupper also mentions Sir Artur Lawson as a precursor of the sport in the South of Brazil. Agnaldo Kupper, "O Brasil Dimensionado Pelo Futebol," *Revista Brasileira De Futsal e Futebol*, 11, no. 43 (2019): 303.

factory would eventually have a major influence on the democratization of soccer after the Bangu Athletic Club was formed in 1904.[3]

Charles Miller was born in São Paulo in 1874 to a British family. His father, John Miller, was Scottish, born in Largs in 1844,[4] and had immigrated to Brazil in order to take up the position of engineer at the British São Paulo Railway Company.[5] He died in Glasgow in 1886, but was buried in Rio de Janeiro.[6] Charles's mother, Carlota Maria Fox, was born in São Paulo in 1850 and married John Miller in 1872 at the Sé Cathedral. She died in 1920 at her hometown and was buried with her husband in Rio de Janeiro.[7] Their son became acquainted with soccer during the 10 years he spent at Banister Court boarding school in Hampshire, England, where he played for his school and where he also played in a few games for Southampton FC (which was known as St. Mary's at the time).[8]

Charles returned to São Paulo in 1894 at the age of 20 with two soccer balls and a book of rules. According to him, upon arrival, his father—who was waiting for him at the dock of São Paulo's port city, Santos—saw the two balls and asked him what they were. Charles responded, "my diploma," and then continued, saying, "Your son has graduated in football."[9] Soon, Miller began encouraging his friends to play soccer, and with the support of the rich British community of São Paulo, Miller established the entire apparatus for soccer to take root in the country. In April 1895, what is believed to have been the first game—based on the rules of the British Football Association—took place. The players were young Europeans, mostly from the UK, who worked in British businesses such as the Gas Company, the London-Brazilian Bank, and the São Paulo Railway Company.[10] Soon after, Miller contacted the São Paulo Athletic Club (SPAC) to ask the club to add a department of soccer. The SPAC was the most prestigious club in the city of São Paulo. It had been founded by British residents in 1876 (or 1888, as some sources have claimed)

---

3 *Revista Piauí*, Edição 75, dezembro 2012 and *BBC News*, October 17, 2013.
4 Ancestry.ca—John Miller's Family Tree.
5 Aidan Hamilton, *An Entirely Different Game. The British Influence on Brazilian* Football (Edinburgh & London: Mainstream Publishing, 1998), 10.
6 Ancestry.ca—John Miller's Family Tree.
7 Ancestry.ca—Carlota Maria Fox's Family Tree and Hamilton, *An Entirely*, 10.
8 Roger Kittleson, *The Country of Football. Soccer and the Making of Modern Brazil* (Berkeley: University of California Press, 2014), 16–17.
9 *O Imparcial*, 21 de outubro de 1927.
10 Mason, *Passion*, 10.

as a cricket club. Soccer would only be included in the club in 1895 because of the influence of Charles Miller.[11]

Miller was instrumental in creating the first soccer league in the country, the Liga Paulista de Futebol, which was formed in December 1901.[12] Only four clubs participated in the league, and SPAC won the first three tournaments. The participants were all clubs from the elites: the Associação Athletica do Mackenzie College, which was founded in 1898 at an elite school in the city; Sport Club Internacional, which was founded by a group of players from different ethnic/national backgrounds in 1899, including the German Hans Nobling, who would shortly break from this club to form his own, the Sport Club Germania; and Club Athletic Paulistano, which had been created mostly by Brazilian-born individuals just before the Liga was founded. All members of the city's upper class, the players, and club organizers experienced *football* as a social activity. It would be only about 1910 that non-elite clubs were able to become involved in soccer, with clubs like Sport Club Corinthians Paulista and Palestra Italia being organized.

Charles's connection to SPAC came naturally, as some of his father's relatives and co-workers had participated in the founding of the club.[13] The club played cricket at Chácara Dulley, a country house that belonged to an English family (most likely his aunt) and also hosted the first soccer game played in the country, in 1895. Chácara Dulley would become the first soccer stadium in Brazil; it was located in the Bom Retiro neighborhood of São Paulo.[14] The club was the great representative of the British community in Brazil, of which Miller was an influential member.

Despite Donohoe's efforts in those early years—and the fact that he was organizing soccer games a couple of months before Miller—the latter is considered to be the leading figure in the development of Brazilian soccer, not only because of the games he organized, but also due to his efforts to consolidate the sport in the country.

Miller was able to do this because he was well connected to the city's elites. This was not the case for Thomas Donohoe, however, who was a skilled artisan, one of the many in this era who had left the British Isles to pursue employment either in the British settler dominions or in other parts of the

---

11 Matthew Brown and Gloria Lanci, "Football and Urban Expansion in São Paulo, Brazil, 1880–1920," *Sport in History*, 36, no. 2 (2016): 79 & 170–171.

12 João Paulo França Streapco, *Cego é aquele que só vê a bola. O Futebol paulistano e a formação de Corinthians, Palmeiras e São* Paulo (São Paulo: Editora da Universidade de São Paulo, 2016), 65.

13 Hamilton, *An Entirely*, 36.

14 Antunes, "O Futebol de Fábrica," 18.

world, including Brazil, where British capital offered opportunities. Working in a textile factory in a faraway suburb of Rio, he lacked the apparatus of elite groups and was socially far removed from the English-Brazilian elite. Miller, however, had been born into the affluent Paulista-British community and also had the advantage of 10 years of private schooling in England. Indeed, right after his return to Brazil, he began working for the Sao Paulo Railway Company, then moved to the London and Brazilian Bank before making a more definite move to the Royal Mail Shipping Company. In 1904 he was appointed Acting British Vice-Consul, replacing his uncle, Percy Lupton. It was an unsalaried post that he held for 10 years. It was at this time that he began working for the Rail Mail, also taking over from his uncle.[15] Miller was, indeed, at the heart of the wealthy British community in his city and well connected to the local elite, such as the Prado family.[16]

The Prados had been involved in politics and business in Brazil since colonial times. In the 1860s, they began investing in the coffee economy, and by the end of the nineteenth century, the family was one of the richest in Brazil. Antonio da Silva Prado was the mayor of São Paulo when soccer arrived. He was the first mayor of the city and served for four terms, from 1899 to 1911. During this time, he was also the president of a few important businesses, including a bank and businesses in the railroad, and meat industries. Prado dedicated his four terms as mayor to modernizing and urbanizing the city as well as to promoting European immigration to the state of São Paulo. Among his investments was the creation of a soccer club, the Club Athletic Paulistano. His mother, Veridiana Prado, also invested in sports, creating the first velodrome in the country in the 1890s, the Velódromo Paulista. This facility would have an important role in the dissemination of soccer and would eventually become the stadium of the Club Athletic Paulistano, in 1900.[17]

One of the key figures in the early years of soccer in Brazil, and one who has not been well examined, especially in the English-language literature, is Antonio Casemiro da Costa, a player at the Sport Club Internacional.[18] He was involved in the creation of the league in São Paulo, working closely with Charles Miller and Hans Nobling. Although Miller was also involved in the creation of the league, it was Costa who became its first president, while Nobling was its vice-president. Costa's role in the early years of soccer in São

---

15 Hamilton, *An Entirely*, 42 & 57.

16 Josh Lacey, *God is Brazilian. Charles Miller. The Man who Brought Football to Brazil* (Stroud: Tempus Publishing Limited, 2005), 157–8.

17 Thaís Chang Waldman, "A São Paulo dos Prados," *Ponto Urbe* (online), 13 (2013): 2–3 & 7.

18 *O Globo Sportivo*, 8 de setembro de 1951.

Paulo was so important that the trophy the league offered to the winners of the São Paulo championship bore his name, Taça Antonio Casemiro da Costa.[19] He was also one of the organizers of the first game between regions in Brazil.[20] Costa had important connections in São Paulo and was a friend of Oscar Alfredo Sebastião Cox, who would become a major figure in the early years of soccer in Rio.

Oscar Cox was born in Rio de Janeiro in 1880. His father, George Emmanuel Cox was an Ecuadorian-British who immigrated to Rio de Janeiro probably in the 1860s. There he married Minervina Xavier Dutra who was Brazilian and with whom he had 10 children.[21] Oscar, like all young men from the upper classes, went to Europe to study. He and Casemiro da Costa began playing soccer in Switzerland when they were students in Lausanne. Cox returned to Rio in 1897 at the age of 17, but it was only in 1901 that he began organizing games after a trip to England where he bought a couple of soccer balls and a book of rules. The very first known game of Association Football played in the state of Rio took place in Niteroi (across Guanabara Bay) at the Rio Cricket and Athletic Association's field. There, in September 1901, Cox and other players from the Paysandu Cricket Club (also founded in the 1870s) played against their hosts.[22] These two clubs would play soccer again twice more, as an attempt to attract attention to *football* in the local population. For example, in October 1901, the newspaper *O Correio da Manhã* stated that it had received an invitation from Oscar Cox to watch the interesting match that was going to take place between Rio Cricket and Paysandu.[23]

The success of these three games gave rise to the idea of playing against a team from São Paulo, where soccer had been established earlier, as we have seen.[24] This first game between states also happened because of the efforts of Costa and Cox. The newspaper *Commercio de São Paulo* described the event as one that attracted the most distinguished families in the region to the picturesque and pleasant compound of SPAC.[25] The popularity of these matches

19 *Estadão*, 21 de janeiro de 2012 & *Veja (São Paulo)*, 10 de março de 2017; and Fernando Atique, Diógenes Sousa, and Hennan Gessi, "Uma Relação Concreta: A Prática Do Futebol em São Paulo e Os Estádios Do Parque Antarctica e do Pacaembu," *Anais Do Museu Paulista: História e Cultura Material* 23, no. 1 (2015): 94.
20 *O Globo Sportivo*, 8 de setembro de 1951.
21 Nogueira, *Futebol Brasil*, 18; and Ancestry.ca—George Emmanuel Cox's Family Tree.
22 Igor Serrano, *O Racismo no Futebol Brasileiro* (Rio de Janeiro: Grupo Multifoco, 2018), 15.
23 *Correio da Manhã*, 9 de outubro de 1901 and Nogueira, *Futebol Brasil Memória*, 15.
24 Nogueira, *Futebol Brasil*, 16.
25 *Commercio de São Paulo*, 21 de outubro de 1901.

continued and, in 1902, games between teams from the two states were organized. In July, two games were conducted at the velodrome and all the players from Rio were members of the Rio Cricket & Athletic Association.[26]

The enthusiasm was such that on July 17, 1902, the Fluminense Football Club was created in Rio. Oscar Cox was its first president and his friend, Luiz da Nóbrega Junior, was vice-president. All the others involved in the creation of Fluminense—including Mario Rocha, Walter Schuback, Victor Etchegaray, and Mario Frias—were from well-off families.[27] Fluminense, which is still one of the main soccer clubs in Brazil, was the second club created in the city, months after the Rio Football Club was formed (although the latter lasted for only a couple of years).[28] Cox played for the club until he moved to Europe in 1910. Also involved in the creation of Fluminense was one of the richest families in Brazil, the Guinles. Three brothers were president of the club: Carlos and Guilherme had their turn from 1912 to 1914, and Arnaldo was president from 1916 to 1931.[29]

Every game at the Fluminense stadium, which was built in 1905, was a major social event in the city, where men and women dressed to the nines and socialized with members of other elite families. In 1911, the newspaper *A Noite* stated that the tea party that was being organized at the Fluminense stadium every Thursday afternoon was a major social success, where "uma linda sociedade" (a beautiful society) gathers.[30] During a match between Fluminense and Paulistano, in July 1905, important politicians—including President Rodrigues Alves and Souza Aguiar, who would become mayor of Rio in 1906—watched a soccer game for the first time.[31] The *Gazeta de Notícias* pointed out that soccer was not only a good way for young men who would influence the future of Brazil to develop discipline, but that it also offered an opportunity for social interaction of Rio's elites.[32] The same notion was reiterated in 1919, when Fluminense played against Flamengo for the state championship final. The *Jornal do Commercio* stated that it was a memorable "meeting" that took place at the Fluminense stadium, with the presence of the country's president, Epitácio Pessoa, and other important authorities.

---

26 *Correio da Manhã*, 11 de julho de 1902.

27 *Correio da Manhã*, 29 de julho de 1902.

28 Serrano, *O Racismo*, 34.

29 João Manuel Casquinha Malaia Santos, "Arnaldo Guinle, Fluminense Football Club, and the Economics of Early International Sport in Rio," *Journal of Sport History* 40, no. 3 (2013): 395.

30 *A Noite*, 1 de agosto de 1911.

31 *Correio da Manhã*, 17 de julho de 1905.

32 *Gazeta de Notícias*, 3 de maio de 1906.

The newspaper also noted that these authorities would get the opportunity to comprehend the importance of soccer for the development of Brazilian society.[33]

A game between these two clubs had always attracted special attention, as Flamengo was created by a group of players from Fluminense who left the latter club after a disagreement. Flamengo already existed but as a rowing club. Soccer was added in 1911 and in 1912 Flamengo disputed its first tournament.[34] A game between the two clubs is still a major classic today, the so-called "Fla × Flu."

Certainly, Miller, Costa, Cox, and other whites from the elite were not the only people responsible for the development of soccer in Brazil—this is a vision that restricted the role of non-elite individuals, who were responsible for the development and popularization of the sport among all classes in the country. However, it is undeniable that the British had a major influence on the development of most sports not only in Brazil, but in many regions of the world throughout the nineteenth century, a consequence of Britain's political, economic, and cultural domination in countries around the world.[35] This would be the reality not only for *football* in São Paulo and Rio, but also for horse racing, rowing, and cricket.[36] The British influence on soccer remained intact for the first two decades of the twentieth century; until 1916, there was always a British team competing in the leagues of São Paulo and Rio. After that time, the only British presence in *football* was that of a handful of individuals.[37] From that point forward, Brazilians took over the sport and it was with non-European individuals that soccer became the most popular sport in the country. Its adaptability, flexibility, and affordability explain this expansion, not only in Brazil but around the world.[38]

---

33 *Jornal do Commercio*, 22 de dezembro de 1919.
34 *Jornal do Brasil*, 8 de julho de 1912; and *Gazeta de Notícias*, 8 de julho de 1912.
35 John G. Reid and Robert Reid, "Diffusion and Discursive Stabilization: Sports Historiography and the Contrasting Fortunes of Cricket and Ice Hockey in Canada's Maritime Province, 1869–1914," *Jornal of Sport History*, 42, no. 1 (Spring 2015): 89. See also Allen Guttmann, *Games and Empires. Modern Sports and Cultural Imperialism* (New York: Columbia University Press, 1994).
36 André Ricardo Maciel Botelho, "Da Geral à Tribuna, da Redação ao Espetáculo: A Imprensa Esportiva e a Popularização do Futebol (1900–1920)," in *Memória Social dos esportes. Futebol e Política: A Construção de uma Identidade Nacional*, org. por Francisco Carlos Teixeira da Silva and Ricardo Pinto dos Santos (Rio de Janeiro: Mauad Editora: FAPERJ, 2006).
37 Hamilton, *An Entirely*, 122.
38 Goldblatt, *The Ball is Round*, 117.

Urban Development in São Paulo and Rio de Janeiro

The Brazilian elite welcomed *football* as a sign of European modernity and as an agent that could help Brazil move toward becoming more the equal of the "civilized" nations of Northern Europe. Although Brazil had never been part of the British Empire—and despite the fact that the British did not make up a major group of immigrants in Brazil—their presence throughout the nineteenth century was significant due to their investments in the country. The British were largely involved in railroads, the production and distribution of gas, public transportation, and electrical energy, along with other sectors, making Brazil quite dependent on British capital. Consequently, Brazil was also an important client for British banks. For example, during the second half of the nineteenth century, Brazil was among the London House of Rothschild's most important clients.[39] The London and Brazilian Bank and the English Bank of Rio de Janeiro were major investors in the Brazilian economy, financing trade, agriculture, and industry. Among British companies in the country, it is worth noting the presence of the São Paulo Railway Company, the São Paulo Gaz Company, Leopoldina Railways, the Botanical Garden Road Company, the Rio de Janeiro City Improvements Company, the Rio Flour Mill (Moinho Inglês), the Clark Shoe Company, and the São Paulo Alpargatas Company, among many others.[40] Britain also supplied most of the specialized labor force for most industries, railroad construction, and other commercial activities.[41]

The interests of these investors were intertwined with those of the Brazilian-born elites. Adopting British sports showed "the affinity of local elites for modernization as well as revealing their desire to reproduce the aristocratic and bourgeois domination of physical culture that the British elites has mastered."[42] It was a relationship that mutually benefited both groups

---

39 Leonardo Weller, "Rothschilds' 'Delicate and Difficult Task': Reputation, Political Instability, and the Brazilian Rescue Loans of the 1890s," *Enterprise & Society*, 16, no. 2 (2015): 389.

40 Francisco Vidal Luna and Herbert S. Klein, *An Economic and Demographic History of São Paulo, 1850–1950* (Stanford, California: Stanford University Press, 2018), 225–6; and Boris Fausto, *História Geral da Civilização Brasileira, III O Brasil Republicano 1, 1889–1930* (São Paulo: DIFEL, 1982), 368–9.

41 Marcelo de Paiva Abreu, "British Business in Brazil: Maturity and Demise (1850–1950)," *Revista Brasileira De Economia*, 54, no. 4 (2000): 389–92.

42 Edivaldo Góis Junior, Soraya Lódola, and Mark Dyreson, "The Rise of Modern Sport in Fin De Siècle São Paulo: Reading Elite and Bourgeois Sensibilities, the Popular Press, and the Creation of Cultural Capital," *The International Journal of the History of Sport: Americas*, 32, no. 14 (2015): 1664.

and one that was also highly personal, with blood ties and kinship groups that lasted until the early twentieth century.[43]

By this time, the predominance of British investments began to slowly decline, while North American capital started to have a presence in Brazil, including from a Canadian-based company that would become the Brazilian, Traction, Power and Light Company, one of several companies founded by a group of American and Canadian investors. The company remained in Brazil until 1979 and was a major lucrative investor in the country.[44] From the very beginning, it supported *football*, especially in São Paulo, as a way to interact with the community and promote an activity that was controlled mostly by English-speaking individuals.

The Brazilian, Traction, Power and Light Company

At the turn of the century, São Paulo was a booming city, one that would soon surpass the capital of Brazil, Rio de Janeiro, as the largest and richest city in the country. The Canadian-owned São Paulo Light Company played a major part in this growth and was a success from its inception in 1899. The investment in São Paulo was so lucrative that the company expanded to Rio in 1904 with the creation of the Rio de Janeiro Tramway, Light and Power Company. The success of these companies led to their amalgamation, culminating in the formation of the Brazilian Traction, Light and Power Company in 1912. This company, which will be referred to as the Light, remained in the country for about 80 years, providing Brazil's two major cities with public transportation, electricity, and telephone service.[45] In 1947, the Canadian magazine *Maclean's* summarized the importance of the company: "You have to go to Brazil to find Canada's biggest public utility." It went on to note that "the huge South American utility is the biggest single corporation in Canada. [...] It is Canada's largest foreign holding, and it is the largest single corporation in Brazil."[46]

Because of its power, the Light was considered to be an octopus, expanding its tentacles into several key areas of public service. It was also criticized for being a foreign company that restricted national competition, often through

---

43 Anne Hanley, "Is It Who You Know? Entrepreneurs and Bankers in São Paulo, Brazil, at the Turn of the Twentieth Century," *Enterprise & Society*, 5, no. 2 (2004): 196–7; and Teresa A. Meade, *"Civilizing" Rio: Reform and Resistance in a Brazilian City, 1889–1930* (Penn State University Press: Hoopla, 1996), 20–21.

44 Barbosa, *Brazil and Canada*, 35, 40–41.

45 Barbosa, *Brazil and Canada*, 30–31.

46 *Macleans*, August 15, 1947. See also: Barbosa, *Brazil and Canada*, 34–6.

bribes and the exchange of political favors.[47] Indeed, developing close relationships with politicians was a key strategy of the Light. When the company inaugurated São Paulo's first tram line in 1900, not only Rodrigues Alves but also Antonio Prado participated in the celebrations.[48] As well, when Prado left city hall, the Light made sure to carve out an excellent relationship with the new mayor, even before he had been inaugurated. Raymundo Duprat carried on supporting the company in the modernization process it promoted.[49]

Criticism arose as soon as the company began to operate in Brazil, however. For example, in 1901, shortly after its establishment in São Paulo, the *Gazeta de Notícias* noted that the "Canadian company Light & Power" was sprawling in São Paulo and "soon will dominate it." The article warned that nobody seemed concerned about the quick spread of the company.[50] In April 1905, an anonymous letter by someone identified as a "Brazilian" criticized the Light for having "full ownership of its concession in Sao Paulo" and that the capital of the Republic could not be in the hands of that foreign company, concluding that Brazil should welcome foreign money, but that Brazil could not sell its soil or freedom. The author was clearly concerned about American imperialism, as they also mentioned the occupations of Puerto Rico and Hawaii and the "situation" in Panamá. They also erroneously claimed that the Light was an American company.[51]

In Rio, the company's intimate cooperation with several representatives of the Brazilian elite was a reality that facilitated its entry into the city, where there was greater resistance.[52] In this regard, Alexander Mackenzie was instrumental. He had been active in the company since the very beginning, becoming its second president in 1915. Mackenzie remained in Brazil, first in São Paulo and then in Rio de Janeiro, for most of his professional life, until his retirement in 1928.[53] He also adapted well to Brazilian social life,

---

47 Barbosa, *Brazil and Canada*, 36–40.
48 *Correio Paulistano*, 23 de maio de 1900.
49 Alexandre Macchione Saes, "Luz, Leis E Livre-concorrência: Conflitos em Torno Das Concessões De Energia Elétrica Na Cidade De São Paulo no Início Do Século XX," *História São Paulo*, 28, no. 2 (2009): 206 & 213.
50 *Gazeta de Notícias*, 15 de junho de 1901.
51 *Gazeta de Notícias*, 1 de abril de 1905.
52 See: Elisabeth von der Weid, "A Expansão da Rio de Janeiro Tramway Light and Power ou as origens do "Polvo Canadense"" (Rio de Janeiro: Fundação Casa de Rui Barbosa, 1989), 2–8; and Duncan McDowall, *The Light: Brazilian Traction, Light and Power Company Limited, 1899–1945* (Toronto: University of Toronto Press, 1988), 143–7.
53 Pedro Tótima, "Alexander Mackenzie," in *Estudos Sobre a Rio Light*, ed. por Eulália Maria Lahmeyer Lobo e Maria Barbara Levy (Rio de Janeiro: Instituto Light para o Desenvolvimento Urbano e Social, 2008), 655.

learning Portuguese fluently and making friends with influential people. The entrance into society in Rio de Janeiro was guaranteed in large part by his personal contacts with leading figures such as President Rodrigues Alves and the city's mayor, Pereira Passos (both were in office from 1902 to 1906), as well as Lauro Muller,[54] who was an engineer and the Minister for Industry, Transport and Public Works during the Alves government and Foreign Minister from 1912 to 1917. Mackenzie's influence went beyond the Brazilian circle, as he was also one of the most influential members of the English-speaking community in Rio de Janeiro and São Paulo.[55]

Despite the criticism, without a doubt the Light was fundamental to the expansion of Rio de Janeiro and, especially São Paulo, where the company arrived at the beginning of a major economic and demographic transformation.[56] São Paulo's population grew from 50,000 in the 1880s to more than 400,000 in 1912 to over a million in the 1930s. It surpassed Rio in size by the 1950s.[57]

The Light also had a major impact in Rio, but when it began to be operational there, the city already had a population of more than 800,000 inhabitants. Rio was also home to federal government offices and had the third-largest port in the Americas (after New York and Buenos Aires).[58] Nevertheless, the Light was also vital in the modernization of Rio. Central Avenue, inaugurated in 1904, was the most significant symbol of this modern transformation. The company not only provided tram lines, but it supplied streetlights, giving Rio the sought-after European appearance.[59] The day after the street's inauguration, the *Commercio de Sao Paulo* reported on the celebrations for the new avenue, pointing out that the "electric trams were completely full."[60] Indeed, streetcars would become very popular in Rio. With the growth of streetcar lines, cities grew and people moved more easily.

The Light encouraged *football* as soon as it entered the country, awarding, for instance, trophies and medals to the winning teams in São Paulo's

---

54 Weid, *A Expansão*, 1; and MaDowall, *The Light*, 167–8.
55 Barbosa, *Brazil and Canada*, 33; and McDowall, *The Light*, 237 & 240.
56 Barbosa, *Brazil and Canada*, 38.
57 Luna and Klein, *An Economic*, 246–7.
58 Bruno Carvalho, *Porous City. A Cultural History of Rio de Janeiro (from 1810s Onwards)* (Liverpool: Liverpool University Press, 2013), 75–6.
59 *Light. Um Século de Muita Energia, 1905–2005* (Rio de Janeiro: Centro da Memória da Eletricidade no Brasil/Memória da Eletricidade, 2005), 11–15.
60 *O Commercio de São Paulo*, 9 de setembro de 1904.

championship.[61] Moreover, the company had a major role in making it possible for soccer to expand from the downtown area, with tram lines growing and serving *footballers*. In fact, the Light and soccer entered São Paulo around the same time and would be seen as positive forces that could bring São Paulo—and Brazil, in general—into the "civilized" world.

The Light and *Futebol* in São Paulo

As noted, the Light was an early supporter of *football*. In 1903, it presented the winning team of the city football championship with medals brought from London. The company also chartered streetcars to transport players and created tram lines specifically to facilitate the access of fans to areas away from downtown. The situation in São Paulo, therefore, which was not repeated in Rio de Janeiro, was that football and the Light grew up together.

In reality, however, the company was not so much a supporter of soccer in São Paulo as it was a supporter of the English-speaking community in the city—a strategy through which it could interact with Brazilian elites. When the Light bought medals to distribute at the São Paulo championship the SPAC (the most prestigious, and British, club in São Paulo) was also the dominant club and the three-time champion of the city's tournament from 1903 to 1905. By supporting soccer, investors from the Light were, in fact, assisting British elite members with whom they shared an imperial affinity. Furthermore, support for *football* was a direct consequence of the solidarity of the British, especially when they lived in a country considered *mestizo* and inferior. Although the managers and Canadian employees of the Light did not play soccer, they wanted to be associated with British culture, and *football* was undoubtedly a celebration of that identity.

In addition, for investors, soccer provided an opportunity for growth. Tram lines that expanded greatly in the early years of operation in São Paulo allowed for greater circulation in and around the city, including for those interested in *football*.[62] After Chácara Dulley was transformed into streets and residential lots, the other two spaces that were used for soccer were the Velódromo Paulista and the Parque Antarctica, both on the outskirts of the city. The Light made these spaces more accessible to fans and players.

---

61 Fatima Martin Rodrigues Ferreira Antunes, "The Early Days of Football in Brazil: British Influence and Factory Clubs in São Paulo," in *The Country of Football. Politics, Popular Culture and the Beautiful Game in Brazil*, ed. Paulo Fontes and Bernardo Buarque de Hollanda (London: Hurst & Company, 2014), 32–3.
62 Brown and Lanci, "Football and Urban," 175–6.

The special chartered trams for the *footballers*, were, apparently, the outcome of an incident that had occurred in 1903. A player from SPAC on his way to the velodrome was arrested for being "dressed for carnival, out of season" and showing his legs in an offensive way. The misunderstanding was solved when the directors of SPAC and the opposing team (the Paulistano) contacted the police and explained why the Englishman was dressed the way he was.[63] It is important to point out that the player barely spoke Portuguese, illustrating the importance of the British presence in the city and the general attitude that many English residents could have toward learning Portuguese.

The Velódromo opened in 1896 for bicycle races but was renovated in 1900 with the intention of offering the best space for all kinds of events, with electric lighting provided by the Light and a facility comparable to the best European venues.[64] With the growth of *football*'s popularity, the space began to be leased for soccer clubs. In June 1902, the *Commercio de São Paulo* noted that never before a sport had adapted so well to "our habits" and that for a game between Club Athletic Paulistano and Sport Club Internacional, the velodrome held 3,000 spectators.[65] In that same month, a game between English and Brazilian players also took place there. The English players were from SPAC and the Brazilian team was assembled especially for the game.[66] The newspaper emphasized the victory of the Brazilians and the civility of the sportsmen, who were young men of the finest education ("rapazes da mais fina educação"). Reference was also made to the fact that the velodrome was filled with the most respected members of the public.[67] *Correio Paulistano* also mentioned another game that took place in the velodrome that month in which "the flower of São Paulo society shone."[68] The importance of the velodrome was also evident in 1903, when a game took place there on the Independence Day holiday between a group of players from Rio, "o scratch-team do Rio," and the Club Athletic Paulistano.[69] Announcements about soccer matches in the velodrome were quite common from this time[70] until the velodrome was demolished in 1915.

---

63 Hamilton, *An Entirely*, 55–6.
64 *Correio Paulistano*, 22 de janeiro de 1900.
65 *Commercio de São Paulo*, 17 de junho de 1902.
66 *Commercio de São Paulo*, 17 de junho de 1902.
67 *Commercio de São Paulo*, 25 de junho de 1902.
68 *Correio Paulistano*, 16 de junho de 1902.
69 *Commercio de São Paulo*, 7 de setembro de 1903.
70 Other exemples: *Correio Paulistano*, 18 de junho de 1902; 25 de maio de 1903; 27 de junho de 1904; 8 de setembro de 1904; *Commercio de São Paulo*, 25 de junho de 1902; 7 de setembro de 1903. See also: Streapco, *Cego é aquele*, 23–7.

The Parque Antarctica was owned by Companhia Antártica Paulista, which would become one of the most important beer and soft drink producers in the country, and was also an important place for leisure and for the sport of soccer. In 1920, Club Palestra Itália (as Palmeiras Athletic Association was known at the time) ended up buying the space and building its own stadium.[71] The importance of the *Parque* was made clear in the city's newspapers, as was the Light's collaboration, which resulted in it transporting players and soccer fans. For example, the first championship in São Paulo, which took place in 1902, was played at the Parque.[72] The following year, the *Correio Paulistano* announced that the Light would provide more tram service between the city and Parque Antarctica for a game between Sport Club Germania and São Paulo Athletic Club.[73] For a game in March 1904, the Light not only provided a very efficient transportation service, avoiding disorganization and confusion, but also provided electric lighting for a charity event performed at the Parque, which included *football* matches.[74] In 1905, the company announced that, "as an experiment, it will make direct streetcars run from Braz [...] to the Parque Antarctica and vice versa."[75] The same happened in June 1908, when the Light ran a "special service of trams for the convenience of the public" when "concerts, sports, football matches, dances etc." were being planned to celebrate July 14th in a "Franco-Brazilian fête" at Parque Antarctica.[76]

The modernization of the city was highlighted by Charles Miller in a letter to his friends in Southampton. He described with pride the development that the Light had brought to São Paulo, with electric trams linking the city and the suburbs as well as producing electricity "by a large waterfall fifteen miles out of town." He concluded that the centre of the city was looking more and more like Southampton.[77]

Exaggerations aside, what Miller was celebrating was the modernization process of the city of São Paulo in the early twentieth century, in which soccer and the Light played an important part. This process was explicitly linked to race and racial identity at a time of pseudo-scientific racism and with the desire of the elites to be recognized as the equals of Northern Europeans. The friendship between the Brazilian-born elites and the foreign residents and their descendants vis-à-vis *football* provided an excellent opportunity to create

---

71 Streapco, *Cego é aquele*, 29–30 and Mason, *Passion*, 54.
72 *Correio Paulistano*, 2 de maio de 1902.
73 *Correio Paulistano*, 19 de julho de 1903.
74 *Correio Paulistano*, 21 de março de 1904.
75 *O Commercio de São Paulo*, 13 de maio de 1905.
76 *The Brazilian Review*, June 30, 1908.
77 Hamilton, *An* Entirely, 42.

a sense of community and camaraderie. In this context, the assumption of superiority was a certainty. Only those who belonged to this special group would be welcomed, and the racial assumptions of these Europeans exerted a major influence on the arrival and diffusion of the sport in Brazil. Soccer provided another way to disempower those considered inferior.

Chapter 2

RACIAL EXCLUSION IN THE GENTLEMAN'S SPORT

Rio's *Liga Metropolitana*

The early history of soccer in Brazil provides a rare illustration of color segregation in a country that has been reluctant to acknowledge its systemic racism. As with the desire to modernize, the influence of pseudo-scientific racism was also a determinant factor in the explicit color discrimination that happened in *futebol*. Brazil never declared any formal policy of color segregation—at least not officially—yet the desire of Brazilian-born elites to be accepted by the "superior races" influenced their attempt at color segregation in the sport, both at the local and international levels. Locally, becoming playing companions of the elite clubs raised the elites' perception of themselves, reaffirming in their own minds that they were not inferior beings. Internationally, the image of Brazil abroad had to be carefully crafted to portray a country of whites—in spite of the perception of Brazil as a racially "inadequate" country, as discussed in the Introduction.

A clear example of color segregation took place in 1907, when Rio's first soccer league banned people of color from playing. The league was created in 1905 as the Liga Metropolitana de Foot-ball, but it changed its name twice, and by 1908 it was known as Liga Metropolitana de Esportes Athleticos. It followed British Association Football rules and emphasized the socialization of members of the elite more than the sport itself.[1]

The league was established with two divisions, the first exclusively formed by elite clubs such as the Rio Cricket and Athletic Association, the Payssandu Cricket Club, the Football and Athletic Club, the Fluminense Football Club, the Botafogo Athletic Club, the America Football Club, and the Bangu Athletic Club. Of these clubs, the first two were controlled mostly by British

---

1 Ricardo Porto dos Santos, *Entre "Rivais." Futebol, Racismo e Modernidade no Rio de Janeiro e em Buenos Aires, 1897–1924* (Rio de Janeiro: MAUAD, 2012), 65.

residents/descendants and did not survive during the popularization of the sport, which was also the case for the Football and Athletic Club. The Bangu Athletic Club, as noted, was inaugurated in 1904 due to the initiative of British immigrant workers at Companhia Progresso Industrial. The Botafogo Athletic Club and the America Football Club were also founded in 1904, but were mostly formed by Brazilians and would be less elite/exclusive than other clubs, particularly Fluminense. For example, the fees to become a member of the latter club were twice as high as those of Botafogo and America and five times higher than Bangu.[2] The Liga also charged affiliation fees, and even for the second division the fees were quite costly.[3] In response, the small clubs had to create their own league, the Liga Suburbana, which was established on May 5, 1907, by clubs from the poor suburbs of Rio.[4]

Liga Metropolitana re-affirmed its exclusivity by passing a resolution, days after the creation of the Liga Suburbana, to ban players of color. The growth and popularization of the sport meant that the elite league had to tighten its separation from the "others." Consequently, on May 18, 1907, the Liga Metropolitana decided unanimously to pass a rule that no individual of color could become registered in the league as an amateur "não sejam registrados como amador nesta liga as pessoas de côr."[5] Alfredo Chaves, a director from Botafogo, protested the decision, pointing out that it was hateful and anti-democratic.[6] Yet, another director from the same club, Cruz Santos, responded that the decision was in fact fair, because the friendship and camaraderie in the sport could only develop between men of the same color and class, clearly implying that Blacks could not be members of the elite.[7] Botafogo, instead of leaving the league, decided to remain and dismiss its only dark-skinned player, Paulino de Sousa, who went to play for a team in the Liga Suburbana. He had not been allowed to stay despite the fact that he played for the second team of Botafogo and appeared only occasionally on the first team as a reserve player in 1906.[8]

---

2 Leonardo Affonso de Miranda Pereira, *Footballmania. Uma História social do futebol no Rio de Janeiro – 1902–1938* (Rio de Janeiro: Editora Nova Fronteira, 2000), 33–5.
3 Pereira, *Footballmania*, 63–4.
4 *Gazeta de Notícias*, 5 de maio de 1907.
5 *Gazeta de Notícias*, 18 maio de 1907. Note: The reference to amateurs is very revealing due to the battle that took place for the professionalization of soccer in Brazil in the early 1930s. This will be further explored in Chapter 3.
6 Pereira, *Footballmania*, 66.
7 Gregg Bocketti, *The Invention of the Beautiful Game: Football and the Making of Modern Brazil* (Gainesville: University Press of Florida, 2016), 79.
8 Pereira, *Footballmania*, 70–71.

The decision in 1907 was a direct reaction to the Bangu Athletic Club.[9] This club had an English tradition, which allowed it to interact with the elites, but it also included non-elite players. By the time the decision had been made, the club was mostly comprised of Brazilian players, although the directors were still overwhelmingly British. Among the players, there were two Blacks: Francisco Carregal, a worker from the factory associated with the club, who played in 1905 in the first official game of the club against the elitist Fluminense; and Manuel Maia, who in the following year participated in Rio's first championship, which was organized by the newly created Liga Metropolitana. When the decision to exclude Black players occurred, Bangu left the league, returning to it only for the 1909 championship.[10]

Due to its acceptance of workers, including Afro-Brazilians, Bangu has been recognized in the scholarship as the first club to attempt to democratize soccer in Brazil. Yet the club did not try to do that when it was created in 1904. As noted above, the Scotsman Thomas Donohoe is credited with bringing football to Bangu in the late 1890s, when he began organizing games with British co-workers from Companhia Progresso Industrial. Yet those members of the skilled working class were not numerous enough to make up 2 teams of 11 players, so they had the option to play with smaller teams (which went against the rules of British Football Association), to invite other British residents of Rio to play with them, or to share the field with others.[11] Bangu was a distant suburb, far from where the majority of the British population lived near the central area of the city, and thus they were unwilling to go there to play. Moreover, they had their own clubs, such as the prestigious Payssandu and Rio Cricket. Thus, the British workers in Bangu had no option but to pick members of the Brazilian workforce to play on their team.[12] Allowing Brazilian-born workers to play was therefore meant to serve the interests of the British founders, not to popularize the sport.[13]

Moreover, anyone who wanted to become a member of the club had to pay fees. Although the fees were five times lower than those of Fluminense, they still functioned to exclude poorer workers.[14] Therefore, there was no intention

---

9 Pereira, *Footballmania*, 68.
10 Serrano, *Racismo*, 62.
11 Leonardo Affonso de Miranda Pereira, "The Flower of the Union: Leisure, Race, and Social Identity in Bangu, Rio de Janeiro (1904–1933)," *Journal of Social History*, 46, no. 1, (Fall 2012): 157–9.
12 Waldercy Caldas, *O Pontapé Inicial. Memória do Futebol Brasileiro* (São Paulo: IBRASA, 1989), 29–31.
13 Caldas, *O Pontapé*, 43.
14 Pereira, *Footballmania*, 32–3.

to bring about a full democratization of the sport. The real democratization happened with the actions of non-elites who created the Liga Suburbana de Football, thereby allowing the growth of clubs in the poor suburban neighborhoods of Rio. The supposed democratization of Bangu happened only because the club would become a powerful advertisement for the factory—becoming more famous than the factory itself, in fact—and it was at this time that any worker who played well was able to join the team, ending the previous racial-socio-economic criteria.[15]

It seems that explicit color segregation at Liga Metropolitana was short-lived, however, as the league changed its criteria from color to profession and literacy.[16] Although no specifics were given, clearly the rule was designed to ban manual workers, who were largely dark-skinned individuals. Controlling the profession of players was a strategy of exclusion that would be present in Brazilian soccer until the beginning of professionalization. In 1916, the Liga Metropolitana specifically pointed out that it could not accept as amateurs anyone who gained "their means of substance from any manner of manual labor," including individuals "who depend entirely upon their physical resources, and not from their intellects."[17] The following year, the exclusion would have a national impact when the rule was adopted by the Brazilian entity ruling sports at the time, the Confederação Brasileira de Desportos (CBD).[18]

The South American Cup of 1921

This exclusion continued, and although no other attempt at official color segregation within soccer leagues took place, the issue reared its head again in 1921, when Brazil's President Epitácio Pessoa (who governed from 1919 to 1922 and who was a promoter of the Europeanization process) and Oscar da Costa (the president of the CBD) met in private and agreed not to include Afro-Brazilian players in the national team competing in the South American Cup in Argentina.[19] The newspaper, Correiro da Manhã, denounced that the president of the Republic did not want men of color in the national team. ("O presidente da República não quer 'homens de côr' no nosso 'scratch.'")[20] It continued, noting that it was a certainty that the Brazilian team would not do

---

15 Caldas, *O Pontapé*, 31–2.
16 Bocketti, *The Invention*, 77 & 268 (note 50).
17 Cited by Bocketti, *The Invention*, 80.
18 Bocketti, *The Invention*, 81.
19 Caldas, *O Pontapé*, 102.
20 *Correio da Manhã*, 17 de setembro de 1921.

well and that the question of color was very detrimental to the good performance of the team. It accused CBD of trying to cover up this racial discrimination, but that it had become apparent that the government of Brazil offered
financial support for the confederation if it kept the national team white. The
newspaper specifically blamed Epitácio Pessoa for the decision.[21]

As the Introduction notes, the image of Brazil was a major concern for
the decision-makers of the First Republic and the image that they wanted
to disseminate: was of a white and "civilized" nation. A sense of inferiority
in relation to Northern Europeans was a reality and a consequence of the
racist ideas of the time. The journalist Gilberto Amado illustrated this sentiment when in 1921 he wrote in the newspaper *O País* that if *football* had been
originally from Brazil, it would have had no prestige, as it was natural for
Brazilians to be ashamed of what was Brazilian.[22]

The South American Cup began in 1916 and was at the time the most
important international soccer event in the region. Before this, the first international event that Brazil had participated in was the Copa Roca, which was
played in 1914 for the first time, consisting of only one game between Brazil
and Argentina. Nevertheless, the event was given significant importance in
the newspapers. For example, the *Jornal do Brasil* identified the team as the
"first Embassy of Brazilian sportsmen" that had left the country in an official manner ("a primeira Embaixada de sportsmen brasileiros que sae do
paiz em character official").[23] It commented that the players selected for the
event came from the most select circles of Rio's and São Paulo's society ("con-
stituída exclusivamente de sportsmen patricios dos mais distinctos circulos
sociaes das sociedades fluminense e paulistana").[24] *Gazeta de Notícias* covered
the event on different occasions and always praised the importance of this
"international" event, the "amazing" match, and the bravery of the Brazilian
"foot-ballers."[25] On October 5, the *O Imparcial* celebrated the arrival of the
victorious Brazilian "foot-ballers."[26] Winning was vital to raising a sense of
self-importance in a nation where the ruling class had to assert itself as equal
to Europeans, or to mostly white countries such as Argentina.

Indeed, winning against a white team provided a sense of pride, as if Brazil
could prove its sophistication through *football*. The year before the Copa Roca,

---

21 *Correio da Manhã*, 17 de setembro de 1921.
22 Milton Pedrosa, *Gol de Letra. O Futebol na Literatura Brasileira* (Rio de Janeiro: Livraria
    Editora Gol, 1967), 162.
23 *Jornal do Brasil*, 11 de setembro de 1914.
24 *Jornal do Brasil*, 15 de setembro de 1914.
25 Gazeta de Notícias, 17 & 28 de setembro; 3, 4 & 5 de Outubro, 1914.
26 *O Imparcial*, 5 de Outubro de 1914.

Brazil won a couple of games against the prestigious amateur English team Corinthians Football Club, and newspapers praised the victories. *A Época* glorified the excellent performance of the Brazilians and the "magnific" Fluminense stadium (both symbols of modernization). It continued by commenting on the lovely atmosphere in the stadium, with no less than 10,000 spectators, including Brazil's Foreign Minister Lauro Muller and many other political representatives.[27]

In 1914, another English team, the Exeter City Football Club, visited Brazil and lost to a team of Brazilians, causing a major sensation. It had first visited Argentina and then played three games in Rio from July 18 to 21. The Exeter team was a professional club (England professionalized football in 1885) and well respected around the world at a time when the prestige of the Southern League, of which Exeter City was a member, rivalled that of the longer-established Football League. It was described grandiosely by *Jornal do Brasil* as the "giants of the beautiful English sport."[28] The club first played and won against Rio's British residents and another time against a mixed team of Brazilian and English players. A major upset happened during the last game, when Exeter faced a strictly Brazilian team and lost 2–0.[29] As *Jornal do Brasil* claimed, the national team behaved "heroically, dominating the violent" Exeter.[30] The defeat reverberated also in Buenos Aires, and when the director of the Exeter stated in his farewell speech that in Brazil there were players who practiced soccer "better, with more intelligence, more agility and more tactic, with more perfection" than in Argentina, a reporter from *Jornal do Brasil* considered this comment to be a second victory.[31]

The sense of pride that began to build up culminated with the club's victory at the 1919 South American Cup. Brazil not only won the Cup, but also sponsored it, the first time it had ever hosted an international event. Although only Argentina, Brazil, Chile, and Uruguay participated in the tournament, it was nevertheless considered to be a large and important event.[32] With the victory over Uruguay, the sense of pride skyrocketed in the country. In addition, Uruguay as well as the other competitors (Argentina and Chile) were perceived as white nations, at least in the South American context, so the victory was also welcomed because of Brazil's need to assert itself in racial terms. Nevertheless, it would not be enough to prevent another racially

---

27 *A Época*, 25 de Agosto de 1913.
28 *Jornal do Brasil*, 4 & 14 de julho de 1914.
29 *Jornal do Brasil*, 20 & 21 de julho de 1914.
30 *Jornal do Brasil*, 22 de julho de 1914.
31 *Jornal do Brasil*, 23 de julho de 1914.
32 *Vida Sportiva*, 3 de maio de 1919.

related incident, this time between Brazil and Argentina, that would have a direct influence on the 1921 color exclusion rules.

In 1920, an important newspaper in Buenos Aires, *Crítica*, published an article linking the members of the Brazilian national soccer team with monkeys. The headline stated, "A GREETING FOR THE 'ILLUSTRIOUS GUESTS,'" and continued, "The monkeys are already on Argentinean soil. [...] We've seen them loping down our streets, doing cartwheels." It also noted that "If there's one group of people that seem truly ridiculous, it's the Brazilians. They are coloured entities who talk like us and try to mix in with the rest of the Americas. It's an illusion." The article claimed as well that a large percentage of European immigrants were "fleeing that country, a country hostile to anything foreign."[33]

The article was accompanied by a large cartoon depicting a group of monkeys, some wearing the Brazilian jersey. The team was arriving from Santiago, Chile, where Uruguay had won the 1920 South American Cup. The Brazilian delegation had to travel by land to the Atlantic coast in order to board a steamship from Buenos Aires back to Rio de Janeiro, and it had been agreed that the team would play an exhibition match with the Argentinean national team.[34] On the day of the game, half of the Brazilian team refused to go to the stadium to play, but the fans who were already there demanded that the game go on. At first, it was decided that Argentinean players would replace the Brazilians (making the team a mixture of Brazilians and Argentineans) in order to avoid a cancellation. The crowd did not accept that makeshift solution, however—after all, the game was supposed to be Brazilians versus Argentineans. The impasse was resolved when the two teams agreed to play with only seven players on each side. Argentina won 3-1 and the media commented on the event as a "riot" caused by the Brazilians.[35]

The incident not only clearly gives evidence of the racism present at the time, but also highlights the racial situation in South America—in which Argentina could much easily portray itself as a white nation due to its small Black population. With racial denigrations of Brazil, Argentina placed itself above the nation and showcased its racial superiority.[36] The difficult interaction between the two countries—which in some ways remains today, at least in relation to soccer—began almost as soon as they began playing against each

---

33 Cited by Jeffrey Richey, "The Macaquitos Affair Soccer, Blackness, and Brazil as Argentina's Racial Other, 1919–1929," *Radical History Review*, no. 125 (2016): 116.
34 Richey, "The Macaquitos," 117.
35 Richey, "The Macaquitos," 123.
36 Richey, "The Macaquitos," 119.

other. In 1916, the Brazilian newspaper *O Imparcial* claimed that the main newspaper in Argentina, *La Prensa*, had always been anti-Brazilian ("sempre primou por seus excessos de anti-brasileirismo") and that it had raised false claims that Brazil would not play in the South American Cup that year.[37]

The author of the article in *Critica* was Antonio Palacio Zino, a Uruguayan who lived in Buenos Aires and who was famous for making inappropriate jokes and comments about players and teams. In fact, he had been a soccer player himself and had participated in the 1919 South American Cup in Rio, playing for Uruguay.[38] Brazil won the final against Uruguay in May of that year and Zino's insults toward Brazil were constant and often alluded to the racial inferiority of Brazilians. On June 29, Rio's *Correio da Manhã* complained that a journalist from *Critica* had published, in Buenos Aires, his impressions from his trip to Brazil, and that all he wrote about were slights. On July 1, 1919, Zino wrote that Rio was "so black that they have to turn on the lights at 4 p.m."[39] In October of the same year, he stated that "Brazil is a country of blacks, and people of color feature in every manifestation of local life," and that the country "gives the impression of going extinct, of a dying race."[40]

The racist comment about the Brazilian national team being made up of monkeys is curious, because the majority of the players were white and from well-off families, making the article by *Critica* even more offensive in the eyes of Brazilians from this level of society.[41] The most apparent exception to this whiteness was Arthur Friedenreich, a mixed-race player of German and Afro-Brazilian background. Yet he could almost pass as white, with his green eyes and straightened hair. Despite the fact that he had been the hero of the 1919 South American Cup, scoring the winning goal and giving Brazil its first win at the championship, he was not selected to play in the South American Cup in 1921.[42]

Friedenreich was the result of an unusual marriage: his mother was Afro-Brazilian, and his father was second-generation German. There is very little information about his mother, Mathilde, who may have been born into slavery, or perhaps was the daughter of former slaves. Indeed, there

---

37 *O Imparcial*, 25 de junho de 1916.
38 Ariel Palacios e Guga Chacra, Os Hermanos e Nós (São Paulo: Editora Contexto, 2014) (Kindle edition), Loc 439, 444, 453, 458, 464, 469, 474, 450 ("O TERMO 'MACAQUITO': MITO OU REALIDADE?").
39 Cited by Richey, "The Macaquitos," 121.
40 Cited by Richey, "The Macaquitos," 121.
41 Richey, "The Macaquitos," 127–8.
42 Martin Curi, "Arthur Friedenreich (1892–1969): a Brazilian biography," *Soccer & Society*, 15, no. 1 (2014): 21 & 24.

is conflicting information about Arthur Friedenreich's parents. His father, Oscar Friedenreich, has been identified by some scholars as a German or as an immigrant,[43] but he was born in Brazil in Blumenau, a city which had been founded by German immigrants in the mid-1800s. There is also conflicting information about the profession of both parents; Arthur's father has been identified as a businessman and Mathilde as a washerwoman.[44] Other sources point out that Oscar was a civil servant, and his wife a primary teacher.[45]

The evidence available shows that it was Arthur's grandfather, Carl Wilhelm Friedenreich, who immigrated from Germany to the city of Blumenau in Southern Brazil. He was born in Brandenburg, Prussia, in 1823; married Wilhelmina Schroeder in 1847; and immigrated to Blumenau around 1850–1851, eventually moving to São Paulo where he died in 1900. His wife also passed away in São Paulo, in 1910. Their son Oscar was born in Blumenau in 1861 but moved to São Paulo, presumably with his parents.[46]

It is likely that Oscar and Mathilde faced backlash from society and from his family for their relationship, with Arthur being born in 1892, only four years after the abolition of slavery. This may explain why their marriage only happened in 1899—a few years after Arthur's birth in 1892 and about one year before Carl Friedenreich's death.[47] To speculate, if Oscar's father's health had been deteriorating prior to his death, it is possible he no longer had the strength to oppose Oscar's marriage. In Oscar Friedenreich's family tree, available at ancestry.ca, his marriage is not acknowledged,[48] although the marriage is recorded as having taken place at Nossa Senhora da Consolação Church in São Paulo.[49]

Arthur, as a reflection of the racism prevalent at the time, straightened his hair before any public appearance and avoided appearing in public with his mother. However, he, unlike other non-whites, was able to enter into the world of *football* because of his father's influence and background. Friedenreich's first club was the Sport Club Germânia, the club of the German community in

---

43 See for instance, Alex Bellos, *Futebol. The Brazilian Way of Life* (London: Bloomsbury, 2002), 32.

44 Kittleson, *The Country of Football*, 26; Curi, "Arthur," 20.

45 Wilson Gambeta. *A Bola Rolou. O Velódromo Paulista e os espetáculos de futebol, 1895–1916* (São Paulo: SESI Editora, 2015), Loc. 462 (Kindle edition).

46 Ancestry.ca—Carl Wilhelm Friedenreich's Family Tree.

47 Ancestry.ca—Brazil, Select Marriages, 1730–1955 and Brazil, Select Marriages, 1730–1955.

48 Ancestry.ca—Oscar Friedenreich's Family Tree

49 Ancestry.ca—Brazil, Select Marriages, 1730–1955.

São Paulo, which was founded by Hans Nobling in 1899. From there, he eventually joined Club Athletic Paulistano, one of the five clubs that formed the elite league.[50]

His career was affected by racism from the very beginning, as a letter he wrote in 1918 illustrates. The letter was published by the newspaper *O Imparcial*, and in it, he challenged a statement from a journalist from a reputable (though unnamed) newspaper who had said, among other things, that Friedenreich had walked "like a monkey in a crazy house" ("como um macaco em casa de louca"), trying to take the ball from his teammates during a previous match.[51]

Friedenreich was not well known—especially internationally—despite the fact that he had been Brazil's top striker, likely scoring more goals than Edson Arantes do Nascimento (Pelé). The only exposure outside of South America came with a European tour in 1925. Club Athletic Paulistano held a successful campaign, winning most of its games in France, Switzerland, and Portugal. In Paris, it played against the French national team. At that game, the mayor of Paris was present, as well as a descendant from the Brazilian royal family—Prince Dom Pedro Orleans de Bragança—and Washington Luis, the president of São Paulo (who would become the president of Brazil in 1926). Friedenreich scored most of the goals—11 in total—and was acclaimed by the Europeans.[52] He was not allowed to play in the 1921 South American Cup because of the racial discrimination described above, however, although the reasons were never stated openly. In addition, Friedenreich did not play in the first FIFA (Fédération Internationale de Football Association) World Cup because of a fight between the São Paulo and Rio de Janeiro leagues, which ensured that only players from Rio could be part of the national team—all white players, it should be noted. In the second FIFA World Cup, in 1934, he was too old to play and he retired in 1935.[53]

Lima Barreto, an Afro-Brazilian novelist and journalist, was openly critical of the discrimination that was taking place and also of soccer more generally.[54] According to historian Joel Rufino dos Santos, Barreto understood that the sport was a product of imperialism, of the "arrogant bank clerks" found

50 Curi, "Arthur," 20 and Kittleson, *The Country of Football*, 26–9.
51 *O Imparcial*, 8 de junho de 1918.
52 José Sebastião Witter, *Breve História do Futebol Brasileiro* (São Paulo: FTD, 1996), 21–2 and Caldas, *O Pontapé*, 97.
53 Curi, "Arthur," 21 & 24.
54 Lilia Moritz Schwarcz, *Lima Barreto. Triste Visionário* (São Paulo: Companhia das Letras, 2017), 10–12 & 136–7.

in downtown Rio.[55] Regardless, the fact is that Barreto openly disliked *football*—according to him, it was a violent and stupid game. He was very critical of its foreign origins and the use of English words to describe the sport. Barreto also condemned the attention the sport was receiving in the media, as he did not understand how it was possible that such a futile and insignificant topic was receiving so much coverage, instead of relevant issues such as public health and education. He even created, with a friend, a short-lived league against soccer (A Liga Brazileira Contra o Football). Although the date of the creation of the league is unclear (perhaps 1918), what is clear is that it was short-lived.[56] In 1922, Barreto declared that despite the fact that his league was dead, he was not, and he would continue to fight against soccer ("a minha Liga morreu, eu não morri ainda. Combaterei sempre o tal de futebol").[57]

Barreto's dislike became a detestation in 1921 with the decision not to send Black players to the South American championship. He declared with sardonic irony that the government should make more cuts to public health in order to continue with its policy of killing the "people" as a way to make Blacks disappear. In this way, the ruling powers could guarantee that Brazilian soccer would remain white. His sarcasm continued when he stated that the *footballers* should not have accepted funds from the government because these funds came from taxes (thus contributed in large part by Afro-Brazilians) and therefore the money was of unhealthy origins ("malsinada origem"). Barreto distilled all of his hatred toward *football* and the discrimination that was taking place by stating "Kill the colored ones soon; and hooray to football, which has given so many eminent men to Brazil! Hooray!" ("Matem logo os de côr; e viva o football, que tem dado tantos homens eminentes ao Brasil! Viva!"). He concluded the article by stating that the national team could rent, for any price, some Englishmen, who could represent Brazil in international tournaments.[58]

Thus, it is clear that soccer had begun explicitly as a sport for a British-dominated elite in Brazil, and even as played by artisans it did not achieve any real democratization. Although some people of color did begin to play the sport, soccer authorities responded by imposing restrictions on working-class participants that were covertly designed to raise racial barriers.

---

55 Joel Rufino dos Santos, *História Política do Futebol Brasileiro* (São Paulo: Editora Brasiliense, 1981), 28–30.

56 José Antonio dos Santos, "Lima Barreto: Apontamentos sobre o football e protagonismo negro no Brasil." *Revista Prânksis*, 1 (jan/abr 2019): 110 and Schwarcz, *Lima Barreto*, 137.

57 *Careta*, 8 de abril de 1922.

58 *Careta*, 1 de outubro de 1921.

Racialized abuse was also common in the writings of major newspapers, so that even a highly skilled player of socially respectable origins, such as Arthur Friedenreich, found his career severely restricted by his mixed-race ancestry. The racial barriers that affected Friedenreich and other Afro-Brazilians would only start to collapse in the 1920s and crumbled in 1933, when soccer became a professional sport. In this regard, the Club de Regatas Vasco da Gama, a club founded by Portuguese immigrants who were also victims of discrimination despite being Europeans, would play a major role.

Chapter 3

SOCCER AND LUSOPHOBIA

The Portuguese as an Immigrant Group and Lusophobia

Club de Regatas Vasco da Gama was founded by Portuguese immigrants in 1898 as a rowing club, with significant success in Rio. A soccer division was added in 1916, and soon the club was doing so well that it began challenging the control of the elite soccer clubs in Rio. Although it would be easy to assume that the elites of Brazil would have no problem with a Portuguese club playing at their level, this was not the case, however. This group, was regarded as unrefined and as the least desired type of European immigrant. The independence process and the large numbers of poor and illiterate Portuguese who arrived in Brazil after 1822 only added to the negative perception. In addition, the European view of the Portuguese as non-white Europeans, a perception defended by pseudo-scientific racism, also influenced xenophobia, in the form of Lusophobia, toward that group.

Although it is a small country, throughout the nineteenth and twentieth centuries Portugal had the highest rate of emigration in Europe after Ireland.[1] It has been estimated that from 1860 to 1930, a total of almost 1.5 million Portuguese emigrated, mostly to Brazil.[2] Indeed, from the early nineteenth century to the 1950s, more than four-fifths of all documented Portuguese emigrants went to that South American country.[3] The exact number is impossible to calculate because of the large flow of undocumented immigrants, especially in the nineteenth century.[4] Nevertheless, from 1890 to 1929, more than

---

1 Herbert S. Klein, "The Social and Economic Integration of Portuguese Immigrants in Brazil in the Late Nineteenth and Twentieth Centuries," *Journal of Latin American Studies*, 23, no. 2 (1991): 310.
2 Joel Serrão, *Emigração Portuguesa – sondagem histórica* (Lisboa: Livros Horizonte, 1974), 40–41.
3 Klein, "The Social," 311.
4 Miriam Halpern Pereira, *A Política Portuguesa de Emigração, 1850–1930* (Lisboa: A Regra do Jogo, 1981), 22 and Rosana Barbosa, *Immigration and Xenophobia. Portuguese Immigrants in Early 19th Century Rio de Janeiro* (Laham: University Press of America, 2009), 37–38.

a million documented Portuguese immigrants entered Brazil,[5] concentrating in large cities, especially Rio de Janeiro. In the 1890 census, Portuguese-born individuals made up 24 percent of the city's population and 68 percent of the foreign-born population. In the early twentieth century, their percentage of the population decreased due to demographic growth (including of other immigrants), but they still accounted for 17 percent of Rio's population in 1906 and 15 percent in 1920.[6]

This massive migration, combined with the perception of the Portuguese as an inferior type of European, caused recurring animosity throughout the nineteenth and early twentieth centuries. A belief in Latin "degeneracy" reinforced the negative attributes attached to the Portuguese, including indulgency, immorality, and indolence.[7] A newspaper in Rio in 1908 explained the Brazilians' seeming lack of discipline as a consequence of the fact that Latins tended to fall into decadence, unlike Anglo-Saxons or Germans.[8]

Thus, the reality has been that since the era of Brazilian independence, the Portuguese have been looked down and, on different occasions, have suffered physical aggression and humiliation. Waves of Lusophobia exploded in the period after independence as fears of a possible restoration of Portuguese rule rose and as a reaction to the increasing number of immigrants arriving from the old colonial power.[9] The animosity was so great that, in early 1841, a warning to the police was published in the newspaper *Diario do Rio de Janeiro* about the possible existence of a secret club organized with the sole objective of assassinating Portuguese individuals living in Rio. Although there was never any proof of the existence of such a club, the fact that the warning was investigated is evidence of the level of Lusophobia present in the city.[10]

Competition for urban jobs furthered tensions, as the Portuguese made up the largest foreign component of Rio's working class.[11] Moreover, a large majority, about 75 percent, were poor, and many were illiterate.[12] This not only exacerbated job competition among the poor, but also contributed to a perception of them being unrefined and unintelligent—a notion that, to some degree, still persists today. In addition, the large number of Portuguese-born

---

5 Boris Fausto, *História Geral da Civilização Brasileira, Tomo III, O Brasil Republicano 2* (São Paulo: Difel, 1978), 100–101.
6 Klein, "The Social," 318–19.
7 *Correio da Manhã*, 2 de novembro de 1907; and Skidmore, *Black into White*, 53.
8 *Correio da Manhã*, 6 de março de 1908.
9 Barbosa, *Immigration and Xenophobia*, 80–90.
10 Barbosa, *Immigration and Xenophobia*, 86.
11 Klein, "The Social," 334.
12 Serrão, *Emigração Portuguesa*, 82.

immigrants involved in the retail trade of the city helped create the idea that Brazilian-born individuals faced unfair job competition in the retail sector.[13] Indeed, there was a concentration of young Portuguese men working as sales-clerks (*caixeiros*). Often, they arrived directly to work in a shop of a relative or family friend and would live and sleep in the store, and the shop owner would become a father figure to them. This control of the retail trade was a leftover from the late colonial period, when Portuguese individuals began moving into this sector as cities began to develop. By the end of the nine-teenth century, the Portuguese owned about half of the retail shops in Rio.[14] Most owned very small food stores that served the poor, and during times of inflation the Portuguese were blamed for high prices, thereby becoming easy scapegoats.[15]

With the installation of the Republic in 1889, waves of Lusophobia resur-faced, as the Portuguese were seen as defenders of the monarchy, and thus radical political groups boosted nationalism by instigating violent anti-Por-tuguese propaganda. One example is found in the newspaper *O Jacobino* (a reference to French nationalists), which stated in 1894 that "the Portuguese is the animal who most resembles human beings."[16] The paper also demanded laws that would reserve the ownership of retail establishments to those born in Brazil, while confiscating properties from Portuguese-born individuals. It even proposed punishments for families that allowed their daughters to marry Portuguese men.[17] Another paper, *O Nacional*, accused the Portuguese of stealing jobs from Brazilians and of robbing them by raising food prices (inflation was high at the turn of the century). This inflamed old feelings and caused xenophobic waves to occur not only in Rio, but throughout Brazil.[18]

In the early twentieth century, anti-Portuguese sentiment reappeared alongside racist attitudes toward Blacks and mixed-race individuals. These all symbolized the backward past that clashed with the efforts promoted by the government toward progress and modernity. Portuguese immigrants were

---

13 João Júlio Gomes dos Santos Júnior, "Jacobinismo, Antilusitanismo e Identidade Nacional na República Velha," *Historiae, Rio Grande*, 2, no. 2 (2011): 117.

14 Steven Topik, "Middle-Class Brazilian Nationalism, 1889–1930: From Radicalism to Reaction." *Social Science Quarterly* 59, no. 1 (1978): 96.

15 Barbosa, *Immigration and Xenophobia*, 54–57, 85 & 113 and June E. Hahner, "Jacobinos versus Galegos: Urban Radicals versus Portuguese Immigrants in Rio De Janeiro in the 1890s," *Journal of Interamerican Studies and World Affairs* 18, no. 2 (1976): 131.

16 Hahner, "Jacobinos," 134.

17 Hahner, "Jacobinos," 135.

18 Skidmore, *Black into White*, 86; and Santos Júnior, "Jacobinismo," 117–18. See also Hahner, "Jacobinos versus Galegos," 125–54.

often referred to by the authorities and in the press as greedy and stupid, or as lackeys, cheaters, and exploiters.[19] In the early 1920s, an upsurge of national-ist sentiment blamed foreigners for Brazil's problems and, increasingly, there was a repression of workers who were mostly Blacks, mulattoes, and poor Portuguese immigrants.[20] In fact, the government of Epitácio Pessoa (1919–1922) was clearly anti-Portuguese and anti-worker.[21] Pessoa was responsible for no Black players being part of the national team at the South American Cup in 1921. He and his successor, Arthur Bernardes (1922–1926), were also supporters of the Ação Social Nacionalista, a federation of about 180 patriotic societies that feared the revolutionary impact of the working-class movement, and which despised Portuguese immigrants.[22] This serves to flag that class tensions and racialized prejudices often went hand in hand, and that repres-sive action against one group often accompanied repressive action against the other.

This was the prevailing mood when Club de Regatas Vasco da Gama began challenging the control of the elite clubs. The general belief was that it was ludicrous that a team of *galegos* (a derogatory term for Portuguese immi-grants) and Blacks could challenge and win against the elite clubs.[23] Moreover, Vasco, despite the fact that it had players of all backgrounds and that its coach, Ramon Platero, was Uruguayan,[24] was referred to as the Portuguese team,[25] reinforcing longstanding anti-Portuguese nationalism.[26]

Club de Regatas Vasco da Gama and the Associação Metropolitana de Esportes Atléticos (AMEA)

This racially and class-based antagonism had been aggravated by the suc-cess of Club de Regatas Vasco da Gama after it added soccer in 1916 to the

---

19 Gladys Sabina Ribeiro, "Viagens e histórias de imigrantes portugueses na cidade do Rio de Janeiro na Primeira República: a trajetória de Floriano Gomes Bolsinha" (Ler História, 51/2006), 166 and 169–71.

20 Topik, "Middle-Class Brazilian," 100; Skidmore, *Black into White*, 174; Ribeiro, "Viagens," 187; and Gladys Sabina Ribeiro, *Mata Galegos. Os Portugueses e os confli-tos de trabalho na República Velha*, Coleção Tudo é História (Rio de Janeiro: Editora Brasiliense, 1989), 58 & 63. See also: Gladys Sabina Ribeiro, *O Rio de Janeiro dos fados, minhotos e alfacinhas. O anti-lusitanismo na Primeira República* (Rio de Janeiro: Eduff, 2000).

21 Skidmore, *Black into White*, 174.

22 Topik, "Middle-Class Brazilian," 98–101.

23 Nogueira, *Futebol Brasil*, 139.

24 Santos, "Revolução Vascaína," 248.

25 Nogueira, *Futebol Brasil*, 138.

26 Barbosa, *Immigration and Xenophobia*, 80–9.

original rowing club.[27] Vasco was aimed at good players, not a surprising move for an immigrant community that comprised small businessmen and working-class individuals. In fact, the decision to create a soccer team came from a businessman, Raul Campos, who owned a store in downtown Rio and was a partner in a furniture factory.[28] The goal at Vasco was to create a competitive and profitable team. Soccer was becoming monetized, although it was still an amateur sport. Vasco's attitude was the beginning of the end of the gentlemanly amateurism and the start of the broader acceptance of the professionalization of the sport.

In 1916, the club began competing in the third division of Rio's main league, the Liga Metropolitana.[29] In 1922, it was promoted to the second division of the league after winning that tournament. Once again, Lusophobic demonstrations took place, with *tamancos* (wooden clogs) being thrown at Vasco fans by supporters of another team of the second division (Vila Isabel Football Club).[30] When Vasco won this championship, it was automatically promoted to the first division. Although this created some unease, it was assumed that Vasco would not go much further and would eventually be demoted back to the second division.

During the 1923 tournament, when Vasco lost a game to Flamengo, there were street demonstrations aiming to humiliate the Portuguese. The crowd ridiculed them by placing a giant two-metre-tall clog in front of Vasco's headquarters and putting onions on the statue of Pedro Alvares Cabral, the Portuguese explorer who claimed Brazil for Portugal.[31] These two symbols, the clogs and the onions, were representative of poor Portuguese immigrants in Rio—the wooden shoes a symbol of someone so thrifty that they would not buy regular shoes in order to save money; and the onions a symbol of the small food stores owned by members of that immigrant group.[32]

Yet, at the end of the tournament, it had become clear that the sportsmen of the elite clubs were the ones humiliated. Vasco won the tournament, becoming the champions in 1923, with a team comprised of working-class

27 Nogueira, *Futebol Brasil*, 140–41.
28 João Manuel Casquinha Malaia Santos, *Revolução Vascaína: a profissionalização do futebol e a inserção sócio-econômica de negros e portugueses na cidade do Rio de Janeiro (1915–1934)* (Tese de Doutoramento, Universidade de São Paulo, 2010), 133.
29 Santos, "Revolução Vascaína," 137.
30 Santos, "Revolução Vascaína," 270.
31 Revista Placar, cited by Fernando da Costa Ferreira, "As Múltiplas Identidades do Club de Regatas Vasco da Gama." *Revista Geo-Paisagem* (online), 3, no. 6 (julho/dezembro de 2004). http://www.feth.ggf.br/Vasco.htm#_ftn
32 Barbosa, *Immigration and Xenophobia*, 115–16.

whites, Blacks, and mixed-raced individuals.[33] Nelson Conceição, for example, was a taxi driver; Silvio Moreira (Cecy) was a wall painter; João Baptista Soares (Nicolino) was a dock worker; and Claudionor Correa (Bolão) was a truck driver—all Afro-Brazilians who were joined by four illiterate whites, including Albanito Nascimento (Leitão), a factory worker who began his amateur soccer-playing career at Bangu; and the Italian-born Domingos Passini (Mingote), a wall painter.[34]

No one from the league questioned Leitão's "amateur" status until he began playing for Vasco.[35] It was also after Vasco's excellent campaign that the Liga Metropolitana began enforcing the requirement that amateur players know how to read and write. This literacy requirement was based on the belief that a working-class person who was illiterate would be unable to afford the leisure time to play the sport at a high level without some form of compensation. Immediately, three players from Vasco were pointed out as being illiterate; although they had played for other clubs in the past, only in 1923 were they forced to prove that they met the literacy requirement.[36]

Vasco was not the first club to recruit non-white players. Chapter 2 described the Bangu Athletic Club and how it became a target for having non-elite players, yet the founders of that club had been British immigrants, not Portuguese. Still, in 1907, as noted before, Bangu also had to fight against racism when the main league at the time implemented a rule that banned Black amateurs.[37]

The practice of non-whites being recruited by elite teams gave rise to one of the most lasting traditions in Rio's soccer: Fluminense's nickname of "pó de arroz" (rice powder), and the use of talcum powder by its fans whenever the team entered the soccer field. The association between the club and talcum powder began in 1914 when, after an unprecedented decision, the Afro-Brazilian Carlos Alberto began playing for Fluminense, the most prestigious club in Rio, after having played for a smaller club, América F. C. It seems that in order to appear lighter-skinned, Carlos Alberto applied talcum

33 Nogueira, *Futebol Brasil*, 139 & 145; and José Sergio Leite Lopes, "Class, Ethnicity, and Color in the Making of Brazilian Football," *Daedalus*, 129, no. 2 (2000): 248 and Pereira, *Footballmania*, 308–10.

34 Caldas, *O Pontapé*, 44; Hugo da Silva Moraes, "Jogadas insólitas: amadorismo, profissionalism e os jogadores de futebol do Rio de Janeiro (1922–1924)," *Esporte e Sociedade*, 6, no. 16 (nov. 2010/fev. 2011): 8; "Primeiro estadual complete 90 anos, e família de campeão abre o baú," *Globo Esporte* 12 de Agosto de 2013; Bocketti, *The Invention*, 95 and Santos, "Revolução Vascaína," 255 & 273 & 283.

35 Santos, "Revolução Vascaína," 272–3.

36 Santos, "Revolução Vascaína," 284.

37 See Chapter 2.

powder to his face before each game due to the insults he would often hear at Fluminense. During the course of the game, he would sweat, and the powder would run, at which point spectators would yell the insulting name pó de arroz.[38]

In 2019, Fluminense publicly addressed the issue, denying that Carlos Alberto had been mistreated by Fluminense fans and that he used talcum powder as part of his after-shave routine. It also claimed that it was the fans of his former club, América, who ridiculed him during a game, as a way to show their unhappiness at him having left for Fluminense.[39] Although Fluminense's objective in releasing this statement was to combat discrimination, emphasizing that the club belonged to everyone, denying the racist beginnings of Fluminense (and all other elite clubs of the time) was a disservice to the fight against racism.

Another disservice to this struggle could also be seen in Vasco's quest to be seen as a club that did not discriminate against its players along either racial or class lines. Although this was true in some ways, it is also a simplification of history and of the racism that existed in Brazil in the early twentieth century. It could be assumed that the animosity the Portuguese suffered in Brazil, especially in Rio de Janeiro, may have influenced the directors of the club to break the socioeconomic and racial barriers of the time. However, there is no evidence that the club made an effort to nurture the talents of young, racialized players. Afro-Brazilians were recruited not to make an equalitarian statement but because they were excellent players who had been spotted in small clubs, and not because they were Blacks supported by Vasco from an early age.[40] One example is Nelson da Conceição, who was the goalie when Vasco won Rio's tournament in 1923. Conceição started playing at the Engenho de Dentro Athletico Club, which was the three-time champion of the Liga Suburbana from 1916 to 1919,[41] moving to Vasco in 1919 and playing there until 1924.[42]

Regardless, the reality is that Vasco became very popular among working-class Brazilians, with an increasing number of fans identifying with its team. The other clubs from the first division could have had a non-elite player, as

38 Pereira, *Footballmania*, 114.
39 *Globo Esporte*, 20 de novembro de 2019.
40 Mario Filho, *O Negro no Futebol Brasileiro* (Rio de Janeiro: MAUD, 2003—4th edition), 120.
41 Walmer Peres Santana, "As Mãos Negras do Chauffeur Nelson da Conceição: futebol, racismo na cidade do Rio de Janeiro (1919–1924)" (Monografia, Bacharelado em História, Universidade Federal do Rio de Janeiro, 2013), 2.
42 Santana, "As Mãos," 3.

was the case with Carlos Alberto, but Vasco's team members were entirely from the working class, which was why it was a threat.[43] Although Vasco's popularity can be seen as a contradiction with what has been discussed about Lusophobia, at the time, the disdain for Portuguese immigrants was becoming increasingly an elite preoccupation, while a broader segment of the population began to identify with the Vasco team—not in spite of, but rather because of, the large number of working-class and non-white players.

The team's popularity continued unabated until the arrival of professional soccer, when clubs were allowed to invest in good players without having to pretend that they were amateurs. In the 1930s, Vasco's popularity then shifted to Flamengo, which hired Leônidas da Silva and Domingos da Guia, both Afro-Brazilians and the heroes of the 1934 and 1938 World Cups. Thus, Flamengo could claim a mixed-race identity without the problematic Portuguese component.[44] Still, Vasco was responsible for pushing for the democratization of Brazilian soccer by incorporating Black, mixed-race, and working-class players as well as through further popularizing the sport.[45] Therefore, it is clear that it was with Vasco that the link between social interaction and *football* ended, in the sense that soccer happened because of the sport itself and the increasing number of spectators who demanded a great, competitive game, not as an excuse for socialization.[46]

What Vasco did was, in fact, to push for professionalization, which became a fact in 1933. Players were chosen despite their race and social class, and the only way for the elite clubs to resist this was to fight to keep soccer an amateur sport. A strategy that ensured that only those who could afford to take time off from work and to pay for equipment and transportation to games would be able to play. As a response to Vasco's victory in 1923, the elite clubs created a new league in March 1924: the Associação Metropolitana de Esportes Atléticos (AMEA). Its founding clubs were Fluminense, Botafogo, Flamengo, America, and Bangu. Other clubs could join if they complied with the requirements, which included the practice of sports other than soccer and facilities for practice and competition.[47] Vasco complied with the requirement of being involved in other sports as it had started as a rowing club, but it did not have its own facility until the Stadium São Januário was

43 Santos, "Revolução Vascaína," 273.
44 Lopes, "Class, Ethnicity," 256.
45 Holzmeister, "A Brief History," 71.
46 Caldas, *O Pontapé*, 73.
47 Santos, "Revolução Vascaína," 326.

inaugurated in 1927. The new league also determined that all players had to know how to read and write well and had to hold a stable job, but one that was not manual or menial—"such as office boys, servants, shoe shiners and drivers" ("taes como de continuo, servente, engraxate e motorista").[48] In this way, the class-based and race-based discrimination that had to some degree remained covert was now out in the open for all to see. The rationale for the rules was to keep the sport amateur, as the large clubs were dissatisfied with the lack of control at some clubs, which were providing a type of informal professionalization, paying players bonuses and providing transportation—and sometimes even housing—thus allowing the poor to become "false" amateurs.[49]

At first, Vasco considered joining AMEA, despite the lack of a stadium at that moment, although this could be resolved by building a stadium or embarking on some kind of arrangement. What could not be accepted by Vasco's directors was the requirement to cut 12 of its players (among which 7 were its best players) because of their professions and level of schooling.[50] Vasco's board of directors acknowledged the low social status of its associates and the "simplicity" of its headquarters, but it stated that nothing justified the humiliation of having to cut 12 players who were not accepted as amateurs; thus, it decided, unanimously, not to join AMEA.[51] This decision was overturned in 1925 before its stadium was built, when AMEA invited Vasco and the club was glad to join, despite the continuing requirements for amateurism.[52] Soccer was beginning to be monetized, Vasco attracted many fans and sold many tickets, and thus the profits gleaned benefited both the league and the club. With the participation of Vasco, 130 percent more tickets were sold in the 1925 championship than in the previous one.[53] Indeed, it was with Vasco that it became apparent that more than simply being entertainment, soccer was a profitable business.[54]

48 Santos, "Revolução Vascaína," 327.
49 Antonio Jorge Soares, "O Racismo no Futebol do Rio de Janeiro nos anos 20: Uma História de Identidade," *Revista Paulista de Educação Física*. São Paulo, 13, no. 1 (1999): 122–5.
50 *Jornal do Brasil*, 1 de abril de 1924.
51 *Jornal do Brasil*, 9 & 16 de abril de 1924.
52 *Estádio São Januário* was built in 1927 and would be the largest in Brazil at the time, larger than that of Fluminense.
53 Pereira, *Footbalmania*, 309 and Santos, "Revolução Vascaína," 346–7.
54 Antonio Holzmeister, "A Brief History of Soccer Stadiums in Brazil," *Soccer and Society* 15, no. 1 (2014): 69.

Amateurism versus Professionalism

As had been true in other regions of the world, retaining amateur codes meant retaining the values and culture of the classes considered to be superior.[55] In England itself, the fear that the working classes would dominate soccer was quite real, and when professional soccer came into being in 1885, there was a forceful reaction from the elite clubs.[56] The defense of amateurism was a consequence of the fact that the sport was based on status and hierarchy—that is, social position was more relevant than the sport itself. With professionalization, players were assessed on merit, rather than status.[57]

In the case of Vasco, even after it was invited to join AMEA, the defense of amateurism continued. Every 90 days, all players who were part of AMEA had to give proof of employment—including the addresses and names of employers and salaries—and the level of schooling achieved, as illiterate players were not allowed. Another measure used was a form that every player had to fill out before each game. In the form, players had to use correct grammar and spelling and were required to provide information about their nationality, place and date of birth, and place of work (or name of school, if a student). Vasco's reaction was to give literacy "crash courses" to many of its players in order to guarantee their acceptance by the league. Working-class players were also given "made-up" jobs at shops owned by Portuguese immigrants. AMEA tried to control this by having its agents place surprise visits to players' workplaces to ensure that they were indeed employed. [58]

The fight against professionalization ended on January 23, 1933, with the creation of the Liga Carioca de Futebol, comprising Fluminense, Bangu, Vasco, America, and the Bonsucesso Football Club.[59] From there, it spread to other regions of Brazil, with clubs that resisted professionalization eventually disappearing, such as the Clube Athlético Paulistano. This club, which had been formed by traditional elite families in São Paulo, resisted professionalization to the point that it created its own league of amateurs, the Liga de Amadores do Futebol, in 1925, a failed attempt that led to the closing of its soccer division in 1929.[60]

---

55 This was the case in Nigeria, during British colonial rule. Phil Vasili, "Colonialism and Football: The First Nigerian Tour to Britain," *Race & Class* 36, no. 4 (1995): 69.
56 Tony Collins, *How Football Began: A Global History of How the World's Football Codes were Born* (New York: Routledge, 2019), 58.
57 Collins, *How Football*, 61–3.
58 Caldas, *O Pontapé*, 83–4.
59 Caldas, *O Pontapé*, 78.
60 Antunes, "O Futebol de Fábrica," 28.

One major incentive in the move toward professionalization was the fact that Brazilians began being hired by clubs from other countries where professionalization was a reality, such as Argentina, Uruguay, and Italy.[61] Anfilóquio Guarisi Marques, better known as Filó, was born in São Paulo in 1905; his mother was of Italian descent. He played for Societa Sportiva Lazion S.P.A in Rome from 1931 to 1937. In 1934, Italy, under the fascist government of Benito Mussolini, hosted the FIFA World Cup—the second to have ever been organized—and Filó was invited to join the Italian national team. Mussolini, in an attempt to boost both nationalism and political support, was very careful to ensure that Italy would have the best team possible, and to this end recruited South Americans who were descendants of Italians. Playing with Filó were also four Argentineans, who became the first South Americans to win the World Cup. Filó would eventually go back to play in Brazil.[62]

Leônidas da Silva was another example of a popular player hired by a foreign club. He went to play for Uruguayan Peñarol in 1933, just before the professionalization of soccer in Brazil. He became the biggest player in Brazil in the 1930s, scoring the only goal for the country in the 1934 World Cup. He was also the hero (along with Domingos da Guia) of the 1938 World Cup in France, where Brazil made it to third place. Both players had left Brazil because of the opportunity to make a living playing soccer: da Guia went to play in Uruguay, then Argentina.[63]

Both also helped to break the exclusionary racial practices of the past, as they were excellent players who conquered the hearts of Europeans. In France, Leônidas gained the nickname of *Le Diamant Noir* and became the first player to endorse a product—a chocolate bar, Diamante Negro.[64] With the cancellation of the World Cups in the 1940s due to World War II, his international career declined, and he retired in 1950. Yet despite breaking barriers, these players faced racism, especially in the beginning of their careers. For example, during a game in 1932, after hearing all kinds of racial insults, Leônidas was sent out of the game, apparently after flashing his genitals to the spectators.[65]

The popularity of players like Leônidas helped cement the acceptance of professionalization. The elites that began organizing soccer in Brazil did not popularize the sport, at least not directly. Indeed, they had no desire to

---

61 Caldas, *O Pontapé*, 60–67.
62 Max Gehringer, "A História da Copas de 1930 a 1970," *Revista* Placar, Fascículo 2 –1934 Itália, 1986, 30 & 40–1.
63 Pereira, *Footbalmania*, 312–13, 326.
64 Kittleson, *The Country of Football*, 40–1.
65 Pereira, *Footbalmania*, 322.

see it turn into the massive sport that it is today.[66] In much the same way, Ramachandra Guha demonstrates that, in India, cricket became popular because of the desire of the local population to play the sport, not because English residents wanted to include them. Most of the colonial clubs were exclusively white until the British left.[67]

It was the people of Brazil who contributed to the popularity of soccer— and who turned *football* into *futebol*. They fought for the right to play and to cheer for their favorite teams.[68] The real democratization of soccer happened because fans demanded victories, so playing well—not a player's racial and socioeconomic background—became the most important factor when assembling a team.[69]

---

66 Collins, *How Football*, 165–6.
67 See: Ramachandra Guha, *A Corner of a Foreign Field. The Indian History of a British Sport* (Gurgaon: Penguin Books, 2014).
68 Caldas, *O Pontapé*, 44.
69 Caldas, *O Pontapé*, 43.

EPILOGUE: THE END OF EXCLUSION BUT THE CONTINUATION OF RACISM

It is clear that the beginnings of soccer in Brazil were discriminatory, with the Brazilian elite being influenced by the ideas of Social Darwinism. Nevertheless, in the 1930s, the country began to go through a transition, moving from a nation that wanted to be recognized as white to one that was proud of its mixed racial heritage. Although politicians would exploit this idea, creating a sense of "racial democracy" that hindered the struggle against racism, the movement was started by artists who wanted to "Brazilianize" Brazil. They questioned Brazilian identity, pushing for the cultural decolonization of the country. Artists such as the writers Mario de Andrade and Oswald de Andrade and the painters Anita Malfatti and Emiliano Di Cavalcanti, among others, organized the Modern Art Week of 1922 (on the 100th anniversary of Brazil's independence) and pushed the country to seek a sense of national identity. As Andrade stated, it was necessary to give a soul to the country and to re-evaluate Brazil within the international context.[1] Their reaction was influenced by the increasing violence toward Jews that was happening in Germany and against Blacks in the United States. For these intellectuals, Brazil had achieved something much better than "whiteness." As Andrade claimed, "The day that we are Brazilians and only Brazilians, humanity will be rich in yet another race, the combination of human qualities."[2]

The movement launched by these intellectuals influenced Gilberto Freyre, who would become "a leading figure in the redefinition of Brazil's racial identity."[3] In his most famous book, *Casa Grande e Senzala* (*The Masters and the Slaves*), which was published in 1933, he defended the idea that the uniqueness

---

1 Sirlei Silveira, "A brasilidade Marioandradina," XXVII Congreso de la Asociación Latinoamericana de Sociología de la Universidad de Buenos Aires, 2009. (Online paper.)
2 "O dia que nós formos brasileiros e só brasileiros a humanidade estará rica de mais uma raça, a combinação de qualidades humanas." Silveira, "A brasilidade."
3 Skidmore, *Black into White*, 190.

of Brazilian civilization was the result of the contributions of three races: Amerindians, Africans, and Europeans. Although his perspective on race relations was a romantic one, he was a major force influencing the idea of racial mixing being a positive force and a reason for pride. Yet, in relation to the Portuguese, it is fair to say that this portrayal of a unique Brazilian civilization did not put an end to many people's misgivings about Portuguese immigrants: a generally negative perception of them continued to exist in Brazil throughout the 1900s.

In 1930, with the inauguration of Getulio Vargas as President, the idea of racial harmony was embraced by the populist politician, who looked to develop a sense of national identity that could unite the country.[4] During his time in power, his government began to celebrate and to sponsor Afro-Brazilian popular culture,[5] including carnaval and capoeira. Soccer, or rather the Brazilian style of *futebol*, was used in this national attempt to promote the uniqueness of the country. Freyre highlighted the fact that Brazilians played soccer as if they were dancing, or playing capoeira. He stated that although Brazilians had learned the sport from the English, they had re-invented it in their own mixed-race style.[6] The transition between British *football* and Brazilian *futebol* has been emphasized by Brazil's historiography and had been remarked on by newspapers as early as 1919.[7] Thus, *futebol* comprised all the uniqueness of the country and could even illustrate how Brazilians could be better than the Europeans—not only in soccer, but in race relations as well.

In the 1938 World Cup, Vargas's government trully embraced soccer by sponsoring the national team, which included Leônidas da Silva and Domingos da Guia, the first Afro-Brazilian heroes of a FIFA World Cup. Leônidas was the top scorer in the tournament, which was Brazil's best result ever—they reached third place, winning against such European teams as Poland and Sweden. The popular enthusiasm for soccer became clear to Vargas when he himself began to receive telegrams congratulating "his" team's victories.[8]

---

4 Vargas governed for nearly a generation. First as chief of the provisional government (1930–1934); then as constitutional president elected by Congress (1934–1937), next as dictator (1937–1945), and, finally, as a democratically elected president (1951–1954).
5 See Lisa Shaw, *The Social History of the Brazilian Samba* (Aldershot, England; Brookfield, VT: Ashgate, 1999), Chapter 2.
6 See *Diário de Pernambuco*, 15 & 17 de junho de 1938.
7 Jonathan Wilson, *Inverting the Pyramid. The History of Football Tactics*, (London: Orion, 2008), 128.
8 Pereira, *Footballmania*, 336.

Thus, with his government's support, soccer became more popular than ever, making it a national symbol of Brazilian identity. Yet this support was directed only toward men's soccer. The same government that allegedly democratized *futebol* in 1941 prohibited women from playing sports that were not adequate to "their nature."[9] Although Vargas had supported the inclusion of women as voters in 1932, his populist dictatorship (1937–1945) was increasingly conservative in terms of gender. Soccer, specifically, was seen as a danger to women's reproductive capabilities and therefore it could have catastrophic consequences for the country if women were allowed to play.[10]

The popularity of women's soccer was embraced mostly by the non-elite clubs. Among these was Vasco, which had created its women's team as early as 1923, following their victory in Rio's championship. The same conservative attitude that excluded Blacks and poor Brazilians was also applied to women. The professionalization of the sport would end the exclusion of the poor and non-whites, but would not bring equality to women. In fact, it can be argued that it was exactly because of the growing popularity of the sport among poor Brazilian women that the prohibition took place, in order to keep the class structure and the patriarchal control of society intact. Vargas's decree was reinstated by the military dictatorship that ruled Brazil in the 1960s and 1970s, revoked only in 1979. Championships began to be organized in the 1980s and a national team was created for the first Women's FIFA Cup in 1988, but a lack of investment plagued the sport, making it become unpopular in a wider societal context (and sometimes even ridiculed) until the early twenty-first century.[11]

The conservative attitude toward women was in direct contrast to the democratization of men's soccer, after the professionalization of the sport. Nevertheless, the end of exclusion did not mean the end of racism. When Brazil lost the World Cup in 1950, despite being the favorite team, race became the preferred explanation for the loss[12]: the media claimed that Afro-Brazilians were incapable of dealing with pressure.[13]

The two players held responsible for the defeat were two dark-skinned Afro-Brazilians: Moacir Barbosa, the goalie, and João Ferreira (Bigode), a

---

9 Brenda Elsey and Joshua H. Nadel, *Futbolera: A History of Women and Sports in Latin America* (Austin: University of Texas Press, 2019), 119 & 135.

10 Elsey and Nadel, *Futbolera*, 140.

11 Sebastião Votre and Ludmila Mourão, "Women's Football in Brazil: Progress and Problems." *Soccer and Society* 4, no. 2–3 (2003): 255–7 & 259.

12 Serrano, *O Racismo*, 93.

13 Lopes, "Transformations in National Identity," 80; Galeano. *Soccer in Sun and Shadow*, 89–90; and Serrano, *O Racismo*, 95.

left-back. They were not the only ones to have made mistakes during the game, but they were the only two who carried the blame of the loss for the rest of their lives. Both Juvenal Amarijo and Francisco Aramburo (Chico) had a major role in the defeat, but Chico was white and Juvenal light-skinned.[14] Barbosa—despite being considered the best goalkeeper in Brazil, and one of the best in the world—was accused by the media of not having the strength to take the pressure because of the inadequacies of his race. The impact of the blame was such that the Brazilian national team did not have another Black goalie until Nelson de Jesus Silva (Dida) began playing as a reserve goalkeeper in the late 1990s, becoming the main goalie in the early 2000s.[15]

These racist justifications for the defeat in 1950 would be unsustainable later in the same decade because of the quality of non-white players, especially Pelé and Manoel Francisco dos Santos (Garrincha), who led Brazil to its first FIFA World Cup in 1958. This World Cup was, indeed, a game changer, but in the beginning of the tournament, the team was mostly white. There was resistance to certain non-white players, including Garrincha and Pelé, due to the continuing assumption of the emotional instability of those from their racial background.[16] Although Pelé had enough attitude to ignore the racism, and never to speak openly about it,[17] he admitted in 2017 that racial insults were present during every game he played, right from the beginning of his career.[18]

Clearly, racism in sports is a reality not only in Brazil, and examples of discrimination is persistently reported in the media, including at the Final of the Euro Cup 2020 (2021) when three Black players who missed penalty kicks for England were subjected to racist abuse on social media.[19] A major difference today, however, is that racism is more openly acknowledged and soccer associations around the world have spoken out against discrimination, creating campaigns and networks (such as Football Against Racism in Europe [FARE]) and Observatório da Discriminação Racial no Futebol) that denounce and demand action against discrimination, instead of hiding and ignoring it as had been the case in the past.[20]

---

14 Serrano, *O Racismo*, 92–3.
15 Serrano, *O Racismo*, 93.
16 Fábio Mendes, *Campeões da Raça. Os Heróis Negros da Copa de 1958* (São Paulo: Shuriken Produções, 2018), 125–6 & 158–9.
17 *GQ Magazine*, 4 May, 2012.
18 *Revista Veja*, 13 de novembro de 2019.
19 See for instance: *The Guardian, January 31, 2013; Correio Braziliense*, 8 de março de 2014; *The New York Times*, April 24, 2021; and *Time Magazine*, July 12, 2021.
20 https://www.un.org/en/chronicle/article/racism-football-football-against-racism-f are-experience and https://observatorioracialfutebol.com.br

BIBLIOGRAPHY

Newspapers and magazines

A Época—1913
A Noite—1911
BBC News—2013
The Brazilian Review—1903, 1905, 1908, 1912
Careta—1921, 1922
Commercio de São Paulo—1901, 1902, 1903, 1904, 1905
Correio Braziliense—2014
Correio da Manhã—1901, 1902, 1905, 1907, 1908, 1921
Correio Paulistano—1900, 1902, 1903, 1904
Diário de Pernambuco—1938
Estadão—2012
Folha de São Paulo—1995
Gazeta da Manhã—1905
Gazeta de Notícias—1901, 1905, 1906, 1907, 1912, 1914
Globo Esporte—2019
Globo Sportivo—1951
GQ Magazine (British)—2012
The Guardian—2013
Jornal do Brasil—1908, 1912, 1914, 1924
Jornal do Commercio—1919
Macleans—1947
The New York Times—2021
Imparcial—1914, 1916, 1918, 1927
Revista Careta—1922
Revista Piauí—2012
Revista Veja, 2017, 2019
Time Magazine—2021
Vida Sportiva—1919

Secondary sources

Abreu, Marcelo De Paiva. "British Business in Brazil: Maturity and Demise (1850 1950)." *Revista Brasileira de Economia* 54, no. 4 (2000): 383–413.

Andrews, George Reid. *Blacks & Whites in São Paulo, Brazil. 1888–1988.* Madison: The University of Wisconsin Press, 1991.

54 SOCCER AND RACISM

Antunes, Fatima Martin Rodrigues Ferreira. "O Futebol de Fábrica em São Paulo." Dissertação de Mestrado em Sociologia. Departamento de Sociologia da Faculdade de Filosofia, Letras e Ciências Humanas da Universidade de São Paulo, 1992.

Antunes, Fatima Martin Rodrigues Ferreira. "The Early Days of Football in Brazil: British Influence and Factory Clubs in São Paulo." In *The Country of Football. Politics, Popular Culture and the Beautiful Game in Brazil*, edited by Paulo Fontes and Bernardo Buarque de Hollanda. London: Hurst & Company, 2014: 17–39.

Arteaga, Juanma Sanchez. "Biological Discourses on Human Races and Scientific Racism in Brazil (1832–1911)." *Journal of the History of Biology* 50, no. 2 (2017): 267–314.

Atique, Fernando, Diógenes Sousa, and Hennan Gessi. "Uma Relação Concreta: A Prática Do Futebol Em São Paulo e os Estádios Do Parque Antarctica e do Pacaembu." *Anais Do Museu Paulista: História e Cultura Material* 23, no. 1 (2015): 91–109.

Barbosa, Rosana. *Brazil and Canada. Economic, Political, and Migratory Ties, 1820s to 1970s.* Laham: Lexington Books, 2017.

Barbosa, Rosana. "Imigração Portuguesa para o Rio de Janeiro na Primeira Metade do Século XIX." *Revista História & Ensino* 6, (2001): 163–177.

Barbosa, Rosana. *Immigration and Xenophobia. Portuguese Immigrants in Early 19ᵗʰ Century Rio de Janeiro.* Lanham: University Press of America, 2009.

Barbosa, Rosana. "Portuguese Immigration to Rio de Janeiro: The Early National Period," in *Tradições Portuguesas/Portuguese Traditions in Honour of Claude L. Hulet*, edited by Francisco Cota Fagundes & Irene Maria F. Blayer. San Jose: Portuguese Heritage Publications of California, 2007: 403–415.

Barbosa, Rosana. "Um Panorama Histórico da Imigração Portuguesa para o Brasil." *Revista Arquipélago.* Açores/Portugal, 2a série, VI (2003): 173–196.

Barreto, Lima. *Feiras e Mafuás.* São Paulo, Editora Brasiliense, 1961.

Bellos, Alex. *Futebol. The Brazilian Way of Life.* London: Bloomsbury, 2002.

Bocketti, Gregg. *The Invention of the Beautiful Game: Football and the Making of Modern Brazil.* Gainesville: University Press of Florida, 2016.

Botelho, André Ricardo Maciel. Da Geral à Tribuna, da Redação ao Espetáculo: A Imprensa Esportiva e a Popularização do Futebol (1900–1920). In: *Memória Social dos Esportes. Futebol e Política: A Construção de uma Identidade Nacional.* Organizado por Francisco Carlos Teixeira da Silva & Ricardo Pinto dos Santos (orgs). Rio de Janeiro: Mauade Editora: FAPERJ, 2006: 313–335.

Brown, Matthew. "British informal empire and the origins of association football in South America." *Soccer and Society*, 16, no. 2–3 (2015): 169–182.

Brown, Matthew & Gloria Lanci. Football and Urban Expansion in São Paulo, Brazil, 1880 1920. *Sport in History*, 36, no. 2 (2016): 162–189.

Bulhões, Antonio. *Diário da Cidade Amada do Rio de Janeiro, 1922* (Volume III). Rio de Janeiro: Sextante-Artes, 2003.

Caldas, Waldenyr. *O Pontapé Inicial. Memória do Futebol Brasileiro (1894–1933).* São Paulo: IBRASA, 1989.

Cardoso, Lourenço. "O Branco ante a rebeldia do desejo: um estudo sobre a branquitude no Brasil." Tese Doutoramento, UNESP/Araraquara, 2014.

Carvalho, Bruno. *Porous City. A Cultural History of Rio de Janeiro (from 1810s Onwards).* Liverpool: Liverpool University Press, 2013.

Collins, Tony. *How Football Began: A Global History of How the World's Football Codes were Born.* New York: Routledge, 2019.

Curi, Martin. "Arthur Friedenreich (1892–1969): a Brazilian biography." *Soccer & Society*, 15, no. 1 (2014): 19–28.

Dávila, Jerry. "Brazilian Race Relations in the Shadow of Apartheid." *Radical History Review* 2014, no. 119 (2014): 122–145.

Dávila, Jerry. *Diploma of Whiteness: Race and Social Policy in Brazil*. Durham: Duke University Press, 2003.

Del Priore, Mary. *Histórias da Gente Brasileira*, Volume 3, República—Memórias (1889–1950). Rio de Janeiro: Editora Casa da Palavra, 2017.

Duarte, Regina Horta. *Activist Biology. The National Museum, Politics, and Nation Building in Brazil*. Tucson: The University of Arizona Press, 2016.

Dyreson, Mark. "Prologue—The Paradoxed of imitation and resistance: the origins of the map os American empire of sports." *International Journal of the History of Sports*, 28, no. 17 (December 2011): 2415–2420.

Eakin, Marshall C. *Becoming Brazilians: Race and National Identity in Twentieth-Century Brazil*. Cambridge: Cambridge University Press, 2017.

Elsey, Brenda, and Nadel, Joshua H. *Futbolera: A History of Women and Sports in Latin America*. Austin, TX: University of Texas Press, 2019.

Fausto, Boris, *História Geral da Civilização Brasileira, III O Brasil Republicano 1 (1889–1930)*. Vol. 1. São Paulo: DIFEL, 1982.

Fausto, Boris, *História Geral da Civilização Brasileira, III O Brasil Republicano (1889–1930)*. Vol. 2. São Paulo: DIFEL, 1978.

Ferreira, Fernando da Costa. "As Múltiplas Identidades do Club de Regatas Vasco da Gama." Revista Geo-Paisagem (online), ano 3, no. 6 (julho/dezembro de 2004). http://www.feth.ggf.br/Vasco.htm#_ftn

Filho, Mario. *O Negro no Futebol Brasileiro*. Rio de Janeiro: MAUD, 2003—4th edition.

Fischer, Brodwyn. *A Poverty of Rights. Citizenship and Inequality in Twentieth-Century Rio de Janeiro*. Stanford: Stanford University Press, 2008.

Fontes, Paulo and Bernardo Buarque de Holanda. "The Beautiful Game in the 'Country of Football': An Introduction." In *The Country of Football. Politics, Popular Culture and the Beautiful Game in Brazil*, edited by Paulo Fontes and Bernardo Buarque de Hollanda. London: Hurst & Company, 2014: 1–16.

Gambeta, Wilson. *A Bola Rolou. O Velódromo Paulista e os espetáculos de futebol, 1895–1916*. São Paulo: SESI Editora, 2015. (Kindle edition)

Gehringer, Max. "A História da Copas de 1930 a 1970," *Revista* Placar, Fascículo 2 (1934 Itália, 1986): 1–45.

Goldblatt, David. *The Ball is Round. A Global History of Soccer*. New York: Riverhead Books, 2006.

Graham, Jessica Lynn. *Shifting the Meaning of Democracy. Race, Politics, and Culture in the United States and Brazil*. Oakland: University of California Press, 2019.

Greenfield, Gerald M, "Dependency and the Urban Experience: São Paulo's Public Service Sector, 1885–1913." *Journal of Latin American Studies*, 10, no. 1 (May 1978): 37–59.

Góis Junior, Edivaldo. "Gymnastics, Hygiene and Eugenics in Brazil at the Turn of the Twentieth Century." *The International Journal of the History of Sport*, 31, no. 10 (2014): 1219–1231.

Góis Junior, Edivaldo, Soraya Lódola, and Mark Dyreson. "The Rise of Modern Sport in Fin De Siècle São Paulo: Reading Elite and Bourgeois Sensibilities, the Popular Press, and the Creation of Cultural Capital." *The International Journal of the History of Sport, Americas*, 32, no. 14 (2015): 1661–1677.

Guha, Ramachandra. *A Corner of a Foreign Field. The Indian History of a British Sport.* Gurgaon: Penguin Books, 2014.

Guimarães, Antonio Sérgio Alfredo. "Racism and Anti-Racism in Brazil: A Postmodern Perspective." In: *Racism and Anti-racism in World Perspective,* edited by Benjamin P. Bowser. Sage Series on Race and Ethnic Relations; v. 13. Thousand Oaks: Sage Publications, 1995: 208–226.

Guttmann, Allen. *Games and Empires. Modern Sports and Cultural Imperialism.* New York: Columbia University Press, 1994.

Hamilton, Aidan. *An Entirely Different Game. The British Influence on Brazilian Football.* Edinburgh and London: Mainstream Publishing, 1998.

Hanley, Anne. "Is It Who You Know? Entrepreneurs and Bankers in São Paulo, Brazil, at the Turn of the Twentieth Century." *Enterprise & Society,* 5, no. 2 (2004): 187–225.

Hahner, June E. "Jacobinos versus Galegos: Urban Radicals versus Portuguese Immigrants in Rio De Janeiro in the 1890s." *Journal of Interamerican Studies and World Affairs,* 18, no. 2 (1976): 125–154.

Holzmeister, Antonio. "A Brief History of Soccer Stadiums in Brazil." *Soccer and Society,* 15, no. 1 (2014): 65–80.

Hudson, Peter James. *Bankers and Empire. How Wall Street Colonized the Caribbean.* Chicago: University of Chicago Press, 2017.

Hudson, Peter James. "Imperial Designs: the Royal Bank of Canada in the Caribbean." *Race & Class,* 52, no. 1 (2010): 33–48.

Jackson, Gregory E. "Malandros, 'Honourable Workers' and the Professionalization of Brazilian Football, 1930–1950." In *The Country of Football. Politics, Popular Culture and the Beautiful Game in Brazil,* edited by Paulo Fontes and Bernardo Buarque de Hollanda. London: Hurst & Company, 2014: 41–66.

James, C. L. R. *Beyond a Boundary.* London, Yellow Jersey Press, 1963.

Kittleson, Roger. *The Country of Football. Soccer and the Making of Modern Brazil.* Berkeley: University of California Press, 2014.

Klein, Herbert S. "The Social and Economic Integration of Portuguese Immigrants in Brazil in the Late Nineteenth and Twentieth Centuries." *Journal of Latin American Studies,* 23, no. 2 (1991): 309–337.

Kupper, Agnaldo. "O Brasil Dimensionado Pelo Futebol." *Revista Brasileira De Futsal e Futebol,* 11, no. 43 (2019): 301–310.

Lacey, Josh. *God is Brazilian. Charles Miller. The Man who Brought Football to Brazil* Stroud: Tempus Publishing Limited, 2005.

Lake, Marilyn, and Reynolds, Henry. *Drawing the Global Colour Line : White Men's Countries and the International Challenge of Racial Equality.* Critical Perspectives on Empire. Cambridge: Cambridge University Press, 2008.

Lesser, Jeff. *Immigration, Ethnicity, and National Identity in Brazil, 1808 to the Present.* New Approaches to the Americas. Cambridge: Cambridge University Press, 2013.

Levine, Robert. "Esporte e Sociedade. O Caso do Futebol Brasileiro." In: *Futebol e Cultura. Coletânea de estudos.* Organizada por José Carlos Sebe Bom Meihy e José Sebastião Witter. São Paulo: IMESP/DAESP, 1982: 21–44.

Levine, Robert M. "Sport and Society: The Case of Brazilian *Futebol.*" *Luso-Brazilian Review,* 17, no. 2 (Winter 1980): 233–252.

Light. Um Século de Muita Energia, 1905–2005. Rio de Janeiro: Centro da Memória da Eletricidade no Brasil. Memória da Eletricidade, 2005.

Lima, Nisia Trindade and Gilberto Hochman, "Condenado pela Raça, Absolvido pela Medicina: O Brasil Descoberto pelo Movimento Sanitarista da Primeira República." In: Raça, Ciência e Sociedade. Organizada por Macus Chor Maio & Ricardo Ventura Santos. Rio de Janeiro: Scielo Books, 1996.

Lopes, José Sergio Leite. "Class, Ethnicity, and Color in the Making of Brazilian Football." *Daedalus (Cambridge, Mass.)* 129, no. 2 (2000): 239–270.

Luna, Francisco Vidal and Herbert S. Klein. *An Economic and Demographic History of São Paulo, 1850–1950.* Stanford: Stanford University Press, 2018.

Mangan, J. A. "Prologue: Emulation, Adaptation and Serendipity." *The International Journal of the History of Sport*, 18, no. 3 (2001): 1–8.

Marques, José Carlos. "Do Complexo de vira-latas à 'nossa' Taça do Mundo." In: *Copas do Mundo: comunicação e identidade cultural no país do futebol.* Organizada por Ronaldo Helal e Alvaro do Cabo. Rio de Janeiro: EdUERJ, 2014: 85–108.

Mascarenhas, Gilmar. "Eletrizando cidades e corpos: o futebol no processo de modernização do Brasil (1890–1930)." In: *Futebol, linguagem, artes e lazer.* Organizada por Elcio Loureiro Cornelsen, Gunther Herwing Agustin, Silvio Ricardo da Silva. Rio de Janeiro: Jaguatirica, 2015: 73–85.

Mason, Tony. *Passion of the People?: Football in South America.* Critical Studies in Latin American and Iberian Cultures. New York: Verso, 1995.

Mattos, Romulo. "Shantytown Dwellers' Resistance in Brazil's First Republic (1890–1930): Fighting for the Right of the Poor to Reside in the City of Rio de Janeiro." *International Labor and Working Class History* 83, no. 83 (2013): 54–69.

McDowall, Duncan. *The Light: Brazilian Traction, Light and Power Company Limited, 1899 1945.* Toronto: University of Toronto Press, 1988.

Meade, Teresa A. *"Civilizing" Rio: Reform and Resistance in a Brazilian City, 1889–1930.* Hoopla: Penn State University Press, 1996.

Meihy, José Carlos Sebe Bom. "Para que serve o futebol?" In: *Futebol e Cultura. Coletânea de estudos.* Organizada por José Carlos Sebe Bom Meihy e José Sebastião Witter. São Paulo: IMESP/DAESP, 1982: 11–19.

Mendes, Fábio. *Campeões da Raça. Os Heróis Negros da Copa de 1958.* São Paulo: Shuriken Produções, 2018.

Míguez, Eduardo José. "Introduction." In *Mass Migration to Modern Latin America* edited by Samuel Baily and Eduardo José Míguez. Wilmington: A Scholarly Resources Inc, 2003.

Mills, Charles W. *Blackness Visible: Essays on Philosophy and Race.* Ithaca, N.Y.: Cornell University Press, 1998.

Moraes, Hugo da Silva. "Jogadas insólitas: amadorismo, profissionalismo e os jogadores de futebol do Rio de Janeiro (1922–1924)," *Esporte e Sociedade,*6, no. 16 (nov. 2010/Fev. 2011): 1–26.

Nogueira, Claudio. *Futebol Brasil Memória. De Oscar Cox a Leônidas da Silva (1897–1937).* Rio de Janeiro: Editora Senac Rio, 2006.

Owensby, Brian. Toward a History of Brazil's "Cordial Racism": Race Beyond Liberalism. *Society for Comparative Study of Society and History*, 47, no. 2 (2005): 318–347.

Palacios, Ariel and Guga Chacra. *Os Hermanos e Nós.* São Paulo: Editora Contexto, 2014 (Kindle Edition).

Pedrosa, Milton. *Gol de Letra. O Futebol na Literatura Brasileira.* Rio de Janeiro: Livraria Editora Gol, 1967.

Pereira, Miriam Halpern. *A Política Portuguesa de Emigração, 1850–1930*. Lisboa: A Regra do Jogo, 1981.

Pereira, Leonardo Affonso de Miranda. *Footballmania. Uma História social do futebol no Rio de Janeiro—1902–1938*. Rio de Janeiro: Editora Nova Fronteira, 2000.

Pereira, Leonardo Affonso de Miranda. "The Flower of the Union: Leisure, Race, and Social Identity in Bangu, Rio de Janeiro (1904–1933)." *Journal of Social History*, 46, no. 1 (Fall 2012): 154–169.

Reid, John G. and Robert Reid. "Diffusion and Discursive Stabilization: Sports Historiography and the Contrasting Fortunes of Cricket and Ice Hockey in Canada's Maritime Province, 1869–1914." *Jornal of Sport History*, 42, no. 1 (Spring 2015): 87–113.

Ribeiro, Gladys Sabina. *Mata Galegos. Os Portugueses e os conflitos de trabalho na República Velha*, Coleção Tudo é História. Rio de Janeiro: Editora Brasiliense, 1989.

Ribeiro, Gladys Sabina. *O Rio de Janeiro dos fados, minhotos e alfacinhas. O anti lusitanismo na Primeira República*. Rio de Janeiro: Eduff, 2000.

Ribeiro, Gladys Sabina. "Viagens e histórias de imigrantes portugueses na cidade do Rio de Janeiro na Primeira República: a trajetoria de Floriano Gomes Bolsinha." *Ler História* 51, (2006): 165–194.

Richey, Jeffrey. "The Macaquitos Affair Soccer, Blackness, and Brazil as Argentina's Racial Other, 1919–1929." *Radical History Review*, 2016, no. 125 (2016): 116–136.

Robinson, Cedric J. *Black Marxism : The Making of the Black Radical Tradition*. Chapel Hill, N.C.: University of North Carolina Press, 2000.

Saes, Alexandre Macchione. "Luz, Leis e Livre-concorrência: Conflitos Em Torno Das Concessões De Energia Elétrica Na Cidade De São Paulo No Início Do Século XX." *História (São Paulo)*, 28, no. 2 (2009): 173–234.

Santana, Walmer Peres. "As Mãos Negras do Chauffeur Nelson da Conceição: futebol, racismo na cidade do Rio de Janeiro (1919-1924)." Monografia, Bacharelado em História, Universidade Federal do Rio de Janeiro, 2013.

Santos, João Manuel Casquinha Malaia. "Arnaldo Guinle, Fluminense Football Club, and the Economics of Early International Sport in Rio." *Journal of Sport History*, 40, no. 3 (2013): 393–401.

Santos, João Manuel Casquinha Malaia e Mauricio Drumond. "A Construção de histórias do futebol no Brasil (1922 a 2000): reflexões." *Revista Tempo*, 19, no. 34 (2013): 19 31.

Santos, João Manuel Casquinha Malaia. "Revolução Vascaína: a profissionalização do futebol e a inserção sócio-econômica de negros e portugueses na cidade do Rio de Janeiro (1915 1934)." Tese de Doutoramento, Universidade de São Paulo, 2010.

Santos, Joel Rufino dos. *História Política do Futebol Brasileiro*. São Paulo: Editora Brasiliense, 1981.

Santos, José Antonio dos. "Lima Barreto: Apontamentos sobre o football e protagonismo negro no Brasil." *Revista Prânksis*, 1 (jan/abr 2019): 103–122.

Santos, Ricardo Porto dos. *Entre "Rivais". Futebol, Racismo e Modernidade no Rio de Janeiro e em Buenos Aires (1897–1924)*. Rio de Janeiro: MAUAD, 2012.

Santos Júnior, João Júlio Gomes dos. "Jacobinismo, Antilusitanismo e Identidade Nacional na República Velha." *História Rio Grande*, 2, no. 2 (2011): 89–106.

Santos Junior, Nei Jorge dos. "O Futebol nos Subúrbios do Rio de Janeiro (1914–1923)". *Anais do XXVI Simpósio Nacional de História—ANPUH*, São Paulo (julho de 2011).

Santos Junior, Nei Jorge e Victor Andrade Melo. "Violentos e desordeiros: representações de dois clubes do subúrbio na imprensa carioca (década de 10)." *Revista Brasileira de Educação Física e Esporte*, 27, no. 3 (2013): 411–422.

Schultz, Kirsten. *Tropical Versailles: Empire Monarchy, and the Portuguese Royal Court in* Rio de Janeiro, *1808–1821.* New York: Routledge, 2001.

Schwarcz, Lilia Moritz. *O Espetáculo das Raças. Cientistas, Instituições e Questão Racial no Brasil—1870–1930.* São Paulo: Companhia das Letras, 1993.

Schwarcz, Lilia Moritz. *Lima Barreto. Triste Visionário.* São Paulo: Companhia das Letras, 2017.

Sevcenko, Nicolau. "Futebol, metrópoles e desatinos." *Revista USP,* no. 22 (1994): 30–37.

Sevcenko, Nicolau. *Literatura Como Missão. Tensões sociais e criação cultural na Primeira República.* São Paulo: Editora Brasiliense, 1983.

Serrão, Joel. *Emigração Portuguesa—sondagem histórica.* Lisboa: Livros Horizonte, 1974.

Serrano, Igor. *O Racismo no Futebol Brasileiro.* Rio de Janeiro: Grupo Multifoco, 2018.

Seyferth, Giralda. "Construindo a Nação: Hierarquias Raciais e o Papel do Racismo na Política de Imigração e Colonização." In *Raça, Ciência e Sociedade.* Organizada por Macus Chor Maio & Ricardo Ventura Santos. Rio de Janeiro: Scielo Books, 1996.

Shaw, Lisa. *The Social History of the Brazilian Samba.* Aldershot, England: Brookfield, VT: Ashgate, 1999.

Silveira, Sirlei. *A brasilidade Marioandradina. XXVII Congreso de la Asociación Latinoamericana de Sociología.* VIII Jornadas de Sociología de la Universidad de Buenos Aires. Asociación Latinoamericana de Sociología, Buenos Aires, 2009. https://cdsa.aacademica.org /000-062/1234.pdf

Skidmore, Thomas. *Black into White. Race and Nationality in Brazilian Thought.* Durham and London: Duke University Press, 1998 (2nd edition, 3rd printing).

Soares, Antonio Jorge. "O Racismo no Futebol do Rio de Janeiro nos anos 20: Uma História de Identidade," *Revista Paulista de Educação Física.* São Paulo, 13, no. 1 (1999), 119–129. https://doi.org/10.11606/issn.2594-5904.rpef.1999.137764

Souza, Glauco José Costa. "Liga Metropolitana x Liga Suburbana. Semelhanças e diferenças entre as competições de futebol no Rio de Janeiro." *Esporte e Sociedade,* ano 11, no. 28, setembro (2016). http://www.esportesociedade.uff.br/esportesociedade/ pdf/es2806.pdf

Stepan, Nancy. *The Hour of Eugenics: Race, Gender, and Nation in Latin America.* Ithaca: Cornell University Press, 1998.

Streapco, João Paulo França. *Cego é aquele que só vê a bola. O Futebol paulistano e a formação de Corinthians, Palmeiras e São Paulo.* São Paulo: Editora da Universidade de São Paulo, 2016.

Sussman, Robert W. *The Myth of Race: The Troubling Persistence of an Unscientific Idea.* Cambridge: Harvard University Press, 2014.

Taylor, Matthew. *The Association Game: A History of British Football.* Harlow, England; New York: Pearson/Longman, 2008.

Tischler, Steven. *Footballers and Businessmen: The Origins of Professional Soccer in England.* New York: Holmes & Meier Publishers, 1981.

Topik, Steven. "Middle-Class Brazilian Nationalism, 1889–1930: From Radicalism to Reaction." *Social Science Quarterly* 59, no. 1 (1978): 93–104.

Tótima, Pedro. "Alexander Mackenzie" in *Estudos Sobre a Rio Light,* ed. por Eulália Maria Lahmeyer Lobo e Maria Barbara Levy (Rio de Janeiro: Instituto Light para o Desenvolvimento Urbano e Social, 2008).

Vasili, Phil. "Colonialism and Football: The First Nigerian Tour to Britain." *Race & Class* 36, no. 4 (1995): 55–70.

Vasili, Phil. *Colouring over the White Line. The History of Black Footballers in Britain.* Edinburgh and London: Mainstream Publishing, 2000.

Vasili, Phil. *The First Black Footballer. Arthur Wharton, 1865–1930. An Absence of Memory.* Portland: Frank Cass Publishers, 1998.

Vianna, Hermano (Translated by John Charles Chasteen). *The Mystery of Samba.* Chapel Hill: University of North Carolina Press, 1999.

Votre, Sebastião and Mourão, Ludmila. "Women's Football in Brazil: Progress and Problems." *Soccer and Society*, 4, no. 2–3 (2003): 254–267.

Waldman, Thaís Chang. "A São Paulo dos Prados," *Ponto Urbe* (online—Revista do núcleo de antropologia urbana da USP), 13 (2013), 1–20. https://journals.openedition .org/pontourbe/781

Weid, Elisabeth von der. "A Expansão da Rio de Janeiro Tramway Light and Power ou as origens do "Polvo Canadense"" Trabalho apresentado no 10° Módulo do Congresso Internacional do Centenário da República Brasileira. Rio de Janeiro, 28.09.1989. Mesa Redonda "Energia Elétrica, Estado e Sociedade." Rio de Janeiro: Fundação Casa de Rui Barbosa, 1989, 1–49. http://hdl.handle.net/20.500.11997/874

Weller, Leonardo. "Rothschilds' 'Delicate and Difficult Task': Reputation, Political Instability, and the Brazilian Rescue Loans of the 1890s." *Enterprise & Society*, 16, no. 2 (2015): 381–412.

Witter, José Sebastião. *Breve História do Futebol Brasileiro.* São Paulo: FTD, 1996.

Wilcken, Patrick. *Empire Adrift. The Portuguese Court in Rio de Janeiro, 1808–1821.* London: Bloomsbury, 2004.

Wilson, Jonathan. *Inverting the Pyramid. The History of Football Tactics.* London: Orion, 2008.

Webpages

http://www.huffingtonpost.ca/2014/09/03/coolest-classescanada_n_5755176.html

https://www.fluminense.com.br/noticia/126-anos-de-marcos-carneiro-de-mendonca

https://observatorioracialfutebol.com.br

https://www.un.org/en/chronicle/article/racism-football-football-against-racism-fare -experience

INDEX

1930 revolution 1

Ação Social Nacionalista 40
Afro-Brazilians 27–28, 35–36, 43, 51
Agassiz, Louis 3
Aguiar, Souza 14
Alberto, Carlos 42–43
Alves, Rodrigues 14
Alves de Lima, José Custodio 5, 18–19
Amado, Gilberto 29
Amarijo, Juvenal 52
amateurism *vs.* professionalism 46–48
AMEA: *see* Associação Metropolitana de
    Esportes Atléticos
America Football Club 25–26, 42–43, 46
American imperialism 18
Andrade, Mario de 49
Andrade, Oswald de 49
Anglo-Saxons 7
anti-Portuguese propaganda 38
Aramburo, Francisco (Chico) 52
Argentina 29, 31, 47
Aryan superiority 3
Associação Athletica do Mackenzie
    College 11
Associação Metropolitana de Esportes
    Atléticos (AMEA) 40–46

Bangu Athletic Club 10, 25–28, 42, 46
Banister Court boarding school 10
Barbosa, Moacir (goalie) 51–52
Barreto, Lima 34–35
Bernardes, Arthur 40
Black(s) 39–40, 43, 51; amateurs 42;
    players 27, 35, 52
Bonsucesso Football Club 46
Botafogo Athletic Club 25–26
Botanical Garden Road Company 16
Bragança, Dom Pedro Orleans de 34

Brazil 1, 3, 30–31; Blacks in 4–5;
    British community in 7; image of 29;
    immigrants in 3, 16
Brazilian Bank 12, 16
Brazilian Commission 5
Brazilian elite(s) 6, 9, 16, 18, 20, 22; clubs
    25, 37, 40–41, 46
Brazilian Review 5, 7
Brazilian Traction, Power and Light
    Company 17–20, 22
Brazilian(s) 7, 15, 21, 50; history 1–2;
    identity 8, 51; society 2, 15; women 51
British culture 6, 20
British Football Association 1, 9–10, 19,
    25
British immigrants 42
British São Paulo Railway Company 10
Buenos Aires 6, 19, 30–31

Campos, Raul 41
Canada 17
candomblé 2
capoeira 2
Carregal, Francisco 27
Casa Grande e Senzala (*The Masters and the
    Slaves*, Freyre) 49
Cavalcanti, Emiliano Di 49
CBD: *see* Confederação Brasileira de
    Desportos
Chácara Dulley 11, 20
Chaves, Alfredo 26
civilization 5–6, 9, 50
Clark Shoe Company 16
class discrimination 45
Club Athletic Paulistano 11–12, 21, 34
Club de Regatas Vasco da Gama 36–37,
    40–46
Club Palestra Itália (Palmeiras Athletic
    Association) 22

Club Athlético Paulistano 34, 46
Clube de Regatas Vasco da Gama 8
color discrimination 1, 25
color segregation 8, 25, 28
Commercio de São Paulo 13, 19, 21
Companhia Antártica Paulista 22
Companhia Progresso Industrial 9,
    26–27
Conceição, Nelson da 42–43
Confederação Brasileira de Desportos
    (CBD) 28–29
Copa Roca 29
Corinthians Football Club 30
Correa, Claudionor (Bolão) 42
Correio da Manhã 32
Correio Paulistano 21–22
Correiro da Manhã 28
Costa, Antonio Casemiro da 12–13, 15
Costa, Oscar da 28
Cox, Arnaldo 14
Cox, Carlos 14
Cox, George Emmanuel 13
Cox, Guilherme 14
Cox, Oscar Alfredo Sebastião 13–15
Critica 31–32
cultural decolonization 49

dark-skinned people 5, 8, 28
democratization 10, 27–28, 35, 48, 51
Diamante Negro 47
Diario do Rio de Janeiro 38
Dom Pedro Orleans de Bragança 34
Donohoe, Thomas 9, 11–12, 27
dos Santos, Joel Rufino 34
dos Santos, Manoel Francisco (Garrincha)
    52
Duprat, Raymundo 18

emigration 37
Engenho de Dentro Athletico Club 43
English Bank of Rio de Janeiro 16
enslaved Africans 2
Época, A 30
Etchegaray, Victor 14
Euro Cup 2020 (2021) 52
Europe 3–4
European immigrants 31
European immigration 3–4, 12
Europeanization 28
Europeans 7, 23
Exeter City Football Club 30

favelas 5
Fédération Internationale de Football
    Association (FIFA) World Cup 1, 34,
    47, 50; 1934 47; 1938 47, 50; 1950 51;
    1958 52
Ferreira, João (Bigode) 51
FIFA: *see* Fédération Internationale de
    Football Association World Cup
First Republic 1–2, 29
"Fla × Flu" 15
Flamengo 14–15, 41, 44
Fluminense Football Club 14–15, 25–27,
    42–43, 46
Football Against Racism in Europe
    (FARE) 52
Football and Athletic Club 25–26
Football League 30
Fox, Carlota Maria 10
Freyre, Gilberto 49
Frias, Mario 14
Friedenreich, Arthur 32–34, 36
Friedenreich, Carl Wilhelm 33
Friedenreich, Mathilde 32–33
Friedenreich, Oscar 33
funding 2
futebol 20–23, 25, 48, 50–51

Gazeta de Notícias 14, 18, 29
Gobineau, Arthur 4
Great Britain 6, 15
Guarisi Marques, Anfilóquio (Filó) 47
Guha, Ramachandra 48
Guia, Domingos da 44, 50

Hawaii 18
historiography 1, 50
Huffington Post 2

Italy 47

James, C. L. R. 7
Jesus Silva, Nelson de (Dida) 52
Jornal do Brasil 29–30
Jornal do Commercio 14

La Prensa 32
Lacerda, João Baptista 4
Latin Americans 5
Leopoldina Railways 16
Liga Carioca de Futebol 46
Liga de Amadores do Futebol 46

Liga Metropolitana de Foot-ball (Liga Metropolitana de Esportes Athleticos) 25–28, 41–42
Liga Paulista de Futebol 11
Liga Suburbana de Football 26, 28, 43
London House of Rothschild 16
London Universal Races Congress 4
Luis, Washington 34
Lupton, Percy 12
Lusophobia 37–41, 44

Mackenzie, Alexander 18
Maclean 17
Maia, Manuel 27
Malfatti, Anita 49
mestizo 20
military dictatorship 8
Miller, Charles 9–12, 15, 22
Miller, John 10
miscegenation 3–4
mixed-race identity 44
mixed-race population 3, 5, 39
Modern Art Week 49
modernity 6, 8–9, 16, 39
modernization 16, 18–19, 22
Monroe Doctrine 5
Moreira, Silvio (Cecy) 42
Muller, Lauro 19, 30
Mussolini, Benito 47

Nascimento, Albanito (Leitão) 42
Nascimento, Edson Arantes do (Pelé) 34, 52
National Congress 3
national discourse 8
national identity 50
nationalism 38, 40, 47
Niteroi 13
Nobling, Hans 11–12, 34
Nóbrega Junior, Luiz da 14
Noite, A 14
non-elite clubs 11, 51
non-elite players 15, 27, 42–44
non-white Europeans 37
North America 5
Northern Europeans 29
Nossa Senhora da Consolação Church 33

O Correio da Manhã 13
O Imparcial 29, 32, 34
O Jacobino 38

O Nacional 38
O País 29
Observatório da Discriminação Racial no Futebol 52
Orleans de Bragança imperial family 2

Palestra Italia 11
Panamá 18
Parque Antarctica 20, 22
Passini, Domingos (Mingote) 42
Passos, Pereira 19
Paulistano Athletic Club 12
Payssandu Cricket Club 13, 25, 27
Pessoa, Epitácio 14, 28–29, 39
Platero, Ramon 40
popular culture 50
Portuguese 8; government 6; as immigrant group 37–41, 46
post-emancipation 7
Prado, Antonio da Silva 12, 18
Prado, Veridiana 12
professionalization 7–8, 44, 46–47, 51
pseudo-scientific racism 22, 25, 37
public education 2
Puerto Rico 18

race 22
racial assumptions 8, 23
racial barriers 8, 35–36, 43
racial democracy 8, 49
racial discrimination 34–36, 43, 45, 52
racial exclusion 1, 25–36; Liga Metropolitana de Foot-ball 25–28; South American Cup (1921) 28–36
racial harmony 50
racial identity 22, 49
racial inadequacies 3, 5
racial inferiority 3, 32
racial mixing 3–5, 8, 50
racialized abuse 36
racism 8, 33–34, 42–43, 47, 49, 52
racist attitudes 39
Rail Mail 12
Rio Cricket and Athletic Association 13, 14, 25, 27
Rio de Janeiro 5, 7–8, 18–20, 25, 31, 38; *see also* São Paulo and Rio de Janeiro
Rio de Janeiro City Improvements Company 16
Rio de Janeiro Tramway, Light and Power Company 17

Rio Flour Mill (Moinho Inglês) 16
Rio Football Club 14
Rocha, Mario 14
Roosevelt, Theodore 5
Royal Mail Shipping Company 12

Saint Louis International Exposition 5
Saint Mary's University 1
samba 2
Santos, Cruz 26
São Paulo 1–2, 4, 7–8, 18–23; *see also* São
    Paulo and Rio de Janeiro
São Paulo Alpargatas Company 16
São Paulo and Rio de Janeiro: early years
    of soccer 9–15; urban development in
    16–17
São Paulo Athletic Club (SPAC) 10–11,
    13, 20–22
São Paulo Gaz Company 16
São Paulo Light Company 17
São Paulo Railway Company 12, 16
Schroeder, Wilhelmina 33
Schuback, Walter 14
secondary education 2
Silva, Leônidas da 44, 47, 50
slavery 2, 33
Soares, João Baptista (Nicolino) 42
Social Darwinism 1, 3, 49
socialization 25
Societa Sportiva Lazion S.P.A 47
Sousa, Paulino de 26

South America 31
South American Cup: 1919 32; 1920 31;
    1921 28–36, 40
South Americans 47
Southern League 30
SPAC: *see* São Paulo Athletic Club
Sport Club Corinthians Paulista 11
Sport Club Germânia 11, 22, 33
Sport Club Internacional 11–12, 21
Stadium São Januário 44
systematic racism 2, 25

United States 4–5
urban reforms 5
Uruguay 30, 32, 47
Uruguayan Peñarol 47

Vargas, Getúlio 8, 50–51
Velódromo Paulista 12, 20–21
Vila Isabel Football Club 41

white colonization and domination 3
white superiority 3, 8
Women's FIFA Cup (1988) 51
working-class players 41–42, 46
World War II 47

Xavier Dutra, Minervina 13
xenophobia 37, 39

Zino, Antonio Palacio 32

9 781785 279249